RESPECT
IN ACTION

‡‡‡

Applying Subsidiarity in Business

Michael J. Naughton

Jeanne G. Buckeye

Kenneth E. Goodpaster

T. Dean Maines

ISBN 978-0-9961691-0-3 (paper)
ISBN 978-0-9961691-1-0 (e-book)

SPONSORED BY
UNIAPAC
International Christian Union of Business Executives

University of St. Thomas
John A. Ryan Institute for Catholic Social Thought
    of the Center for Catholic Studies
Veritas Institute of the Opus College of Business

RESPECT IN ACTION

CONTENTS

ACKNOWLEDGMENTS

THIS ESSAY WAS WRITTEN FOR UNIAPAC, an International Christian business organization that fosters the integration of faith, ethics, and business practice. The purpose of this essay expands and develops the discussion of subsidiarity found in the *Vocation of the Business Leader* issued by the Pontifical Council for Justice and Peace. Pati Provinske, research assistant to the Koch Chair in Business Ethics of the Opus College of Business, provided significant assistance with editing and research and she has created an Annotated Bibliography that serves as a rich resource for further research on the principle of subsidiarity, (http://www.stthomas.edu/cathstudies/cst/research/publications/subsidiarity). Mary Child and Elizabeth Kelly were invaluable in editing the paper. We have received very helpful comments and criticisms on the paper from Juan Jesus Alvarez, Anthony Brenninkmeyer, Bill Brinkmann, Loraine Brown, André Delbecq, Michel-Thierry Dupont, Ron Duska, Dan Dwyer, Bruno Dyck, Neil Hamilton, Robert Kennedy, Daryl Koehn, Terrance McGoldrick, Sr. Maureen McGuire, Domènec Melé, Jim Mitchell, Ed Mosel, Celeste Mueller, John Mundell, Dan O'Brien, Kyle Smith, Mark Taylor, Bob Wahlstedt, and Patricia Werhane. We are particularly grateful to Pierre Lecocq from UNIAPAC who first suggested this project and whose extensive comments have guided the structure and tone of this paper.

FOREWORD

THE ECONOMY OF THE PAST CENTURY was based on a sophisticated division of labor. In order for it to develop, it required entrepreneurs, companies, and business leaders with the capacity to organize, coordinate, innovate, and take risks. This economic model gave rise to a tremendous increase in productivity and progress in terms of civilization. In the past two hundred years, it has brought about unprecedented economic growth and, with it, numerous challenges for society.

The role of leaders in business is evolving in exciting new ways. We must help bring about a sustainable, inclusive economy where the overall prosperity of our culture is based on the development of human dignity.

UNIAPAC has been an important part of this ongoing evolution. In 2008, we published "The Profit of Values," describing a model for Corporate Social Responsibility (CSR) that focuses on the flourishing of the human person. Based on values, this model invokes true change in business attitudes and has tremendous potential to bring about more responsible and sustainable economic, social, and human progress.

A few years later, we released the "CSR Protocol: A Comprehensive Corporate Management Guide" in order to support the implementation process of the concepts found within "The Profit of Values."

As a continuation of our efforts to promote our aim and vision, and to support other committed business leaders with similar goals, UNIAPAC, together with the John A. Ryan Institute, have now gone a step further to completing this implementation process. This book, *Respect in Action: Applying Subsidiarity in Business*, will help us foster a new leadership style focused on promoting the integral development of the human person. By introducing and discussing this practical leadership, we hope to usher in a form of management that respects the dignity of the human person, thereby creating sustainable conditions that will ensure the success of companies and their stakeholders.

I would like to express my heartfelt thanks and congratulations to Michael Naughton and his team, as well as Pierre Lecocq, for the important contributions they are making to the business community.

José M. Simone
UNIAPAC President
Buenos Aires
January 2015

PREFACE

I HAVE BEEN A BUSINESSMAN for more than forty years. For much of this time, I have drawn counsel and wisdom from a community of international business leaders originally called *Union Internationale des Associations Patronales Catholiques*, or UNIAPAC. Established in Europe in 1931, UNIAPAC is an association of Christian business leaders with members from thirty-seven countries around the world. Inspired by the social teachings of the Christian churches, UNIAPAC's mission is to promote a vision of business built on the dignity and respect of the human person and the promotion of the common good.

In 2008, under my Mexican friend Jose Ignacio Mariscal's presidency, UNIAPAC formalized its vision of businesses within human societies. It published a document on corporate social responsibility (hereafter CSR) entitled "The Profit of Values." Anchoring CSR in the respect of basic human needs, the document avoids the trap of making CSR just another instrumentalizing management tool. It was translated into seven languages for our worldwide associations and eventually led to a training corpus called "The Protocol" that is now being used to train hundreds of business leaders in Latin America and Africa. This training tool was built by our Latin America region under the very active leadership of Jose Maria Simone from Argentina, who succeeded me as UNIAPAC President.

In 2009, when I became president of UNIAPAC, I built upon the work of my predecessor by focusing on employees as key stakeholders of companies. My own experience as CEO of two global businesses led me to articulate an underlying core management philosophy, which takes special notice of the relationship between management and employees. It was very clear to me that the *principle of subsidiarity* was critically important to the foundation of this project.

Management practices based on the dignity of the human person create conditions for integral personal development of employees as persons. In doing so, they also create lasting success for companies because respected employees—those who have been entrusted with the agile deployment of their creativity—are best able to adapt to the ever-evolving and complex demands of the business world.

Unfortunately, there can be a temptation to judge the examples we have of businesses that create "good work" as either episodic illustrations of exemplary personalities or as sophisticated programs that instrumentalize employees to simply maximize shareholder wealth. When they are the latter, and businesses restructure, for example, through plant closures, layoffs, and the like, these examples can be perceived as better alternatives to wealth maximization. There are times, of course, when plant closures and layoffs are necessary, and I have been involved in my fair share of them. Leaders of business must deliver financial results. As CEO of an important subsidiary of a publicly traded company, an important part of my responsibility is a financial one. Yet, over the last twenty-five years the "financialization" of business and its quarterly result "dictates" have created pressures within business to see financial returns as the *only* responsibility of the CEO. This financial fixation has had the effect of reducing employees from human beings with eternal value endowed with unique individual gifts to mere instruments to be used purely for economic gain whatever the means or method. This instrumental logic is strong and seductive, and as CEO I have found myself caught up in its creeping rationale that detaches us from the deepest expressions that subsidiarity can give us.

Following our CSR "Profit of Values" work, UNIAPAC came to believe that we needed to formalize our vision of management—one that has *at the core of its understanding and action the paramount dignity of the human person.* We hoped that this vision could then lead to practical training tools, such as we created with the CSR Protocol, tools that would serve our associations worldwide and any business leader seeking a management style that resulted in the celebration of human dignity and human flourishing alongside financial return. We wanted to anchor this style of management in the operating principles of the social teachings of the Christian churches. The principle of subsidiarity, a key element of the social doctrine of the Catholic Church, became the foundation on which we would construct our ideas.

But this approach was not without controversy and initiated vital debate among our membership. For some, subsidiarity was too idealistic for the complex realities we all faced in the daily life of business. Some of our members held the opinion that businesses could only thrive with a strong top-down management approach, but they also believed that this approach could successfully integrate respect for the human dignity of employees. (We will revisit this debate in a moment.) Eventually we came to agreement that subsidiarity was indeed an important principle to structure our vision of a management style that respected the dignity of all employees and helped business leaders who were seeking guidance in their search for an authentic, successful, and humane approach to management.

In light of my own experience as the CEO of a global company, I issued a note to the UNIAPAC board explaining how I used the subsidiarity principle to build a successful management approach that could be applied across cultures, races, religions, and nationalities, and yet speaks to the universal spiritual desire of every businessperson and employee we knew: to flourish as human beings in our work. Over time, it also proved a powerful means to creating a culture of dynamism and agility, and this was key to our collective success in even the most competitive business environment.

As practical as my experience was, however, I knew we needed to go beyond anecdotal evidence and test this concept against the intellectual rigor of scholars. About this time, I had the unique opportunity to collaborate with just such a group of scholars and other business leaders. Together we wrote the *Vocation of the Business Leader*, a project initiated and directed by the Pontifical Council of Justice and Peace. This document not only defined the vocation of business leaders in its most Christian sensibility, but it also helped to identify practical recommendations for embodying the principle of subsidiarity for business leaders. Working together on this document created the initial relationship with UNIAPAC and the John A. Ryan Institute for Catholic Social Thought of the Center for Catholic Studies at the University of St. Thomas, and in particular with its director, Dr. Michael J. Naughton, a relationship I am delighted to say has grown and expanded. Mike and his colleagues readily accepted the invitation to work together, and I am grateful for their thoughtful and warm collaboration. I am also particularly indebted to my friend and consultant Vincent Lenhardt, and to Professor Andre Habisch of the Katholische Universität Eichstatt in Ingolstadt, Germany, who helped me to structure our initial thoughts for this reflection.

This talented alliance brought about the rigorous scholarship we wanted, including the compiling of a rich and detailed annotated bibliography. It deepened our analysis on a wide variety of issues, and four in particular that I will examine in greater detail. They are: 1) moral judgment on business practices; 2) the contingent aspect of management practices; 3) the coupling of subsidiarity with solidarity; and 4) the interplay of risk and trust between leader and employee.

Moral Judgment vs. Being Judgmental. First, in the process of drafting this essay on subsidiarity, I had a significant dialogue with Mike and his coauthors over the use of the phrase "moral judgment" and its application to management practices. As practitioners—and I was particularly sensitive to this—we know how often business is not a clear black and white affair. As any businessperson knows, when people are involved, we sometimes fall into a gray zone when making choices and decisions on behalf of our business. Furthermore, tough decisions have to be made in business every day, and while necessary, they are also sometimes painful. Being "moral" does not mean avoiding such tough decisions, far from it. But sometimes, the troubling truth is that, as business leaders, we are tempted to manipulate facts or conceal some of them. We might be tempted—even with noble intentions—to force our opinions and ideas on others who disagree with us. We may even lose our tempers—and professionalism—from time to time. All of this can lead us to foster forceful top-down approaches to management and leadership. As beautiful and good and true as the principle of subsidiarity may be, and however mightily it may call to our deepest hearts, we are still human and we fall short of practicing this principle perfectly. It is an ancient and most human concern, just as St. Paul reminds us in the Gospel: we do that which we do not want to do; the spirit is willing but the flesh is weak (Rom 7:15–19).

Our dialogue over these concerns generated an important distinction between expressing a *moral judgment* and *being judgmental*. As expressed in this document, confusing the two comes "at the cost of abdicating responsibility for using our minds to form well-reasoned judgments about the moral quality of behaviors, our own and others" (§10). As management is essentially about behavior, we cannot escape the moral aspect of management practices. There is no value-free zone in business or any human endeavor. Our responsibility is indeed to form "well-reasoned judgments" about our management practices as we have no hesitation to form such judgments on external business practices. We hope that this essay will help us all to become more sensitive to the moral dimension of management. Awareness of this dimension we trust will lead to the development of more respectful, effective, and inclusive management styles.

Contingency. Second, and related to the concerns above, our conversations deepened our understanding of the contingent aspect of management, even when it is deeply guided by the respect for persons and the principle of subsidiarity. Indeed external constraints or even internal failures may lead top management to intervene more directly in business decisions than they might normally choose to do, and this intervention could appear to employees as a breach of trust, which subsidiarity is meant to foster. Understandably, this potential obstacle was one of the reasons some of our members initially rejected the notion of subsidiarity as proper to business.

In 2008 and 2009, in order to survive the severe global financial crisis at hand, I had to impose a more top-down approach in managing my business than I might have done in a more stable economic climate. And, as might be expected, the first reactions of my employees were indeed a lack of understanding and the corrosive fear that can accompany it. I was perceived as going against the very principle I had been promoting for years. This example from my own business life led us to in-depth discussions about one key aspect of subsidiarity: the limits of the domain of full autonomy. It became my goal that every employee understand that there are limits to the autonomy employees can be given in certain situations, and these limits are defined by the impact their decisions can have on others and the business as a whole. As such, these limits are contingent on the external environment and adapting to them is not a breach of trust but a proper ordering of responsibility. Helping everyone to understand this principle of limitation and autonomy was very difficult at times, but eventually the whole management chain and their operators gained a much needed and much better understanding of what subsidiarity is and what the role of management is while in subsidiarity mode and in times of crisis. The credibility of the principle of subsidiarity began to grow and was much more firmly established particularly within middle management, who had been initially skeptical of this approach.

In Relationship to Solidarity. Third, the authors brought forward this significant principle: the very simple, though very deep, assertion that *subsidiarity without solidarity* leads to individualism and localism, while *solidarity without subsidiarity* leads to paternalism and centralization. As they so eloquently remind us: "Solidarity signals the social dimension of the person while subsidiarity signals the personal dimension of societies.... Mutually informed, each by the other, subsidiarity and solidarity create a synergy capable of supporting authentic, integral human development" (§60).

Risk and Trust. Last, and what I find to be one of the most important insights of subsidiarity is this: the character or quality of the relationship between trust and risk necessary to operationalize subsidiarity. Subsidiarity points to the personal dignity of employees by recognizing that they have the call and capacity to give something of themselves to others. When leaders embrace subsidiarity, they acknowledge that there are risks associated with inviting people to use their gifts according to their own judgment. The importance of taking on this risk is what makes subsidiarity different from delegation. One who delegates confers power, but can, albeit at the risk of losing trust, take it back at any time. In such a situation, employees are not called to the same level of excellence and participation as in a situation governed by the principle of subsidiarity, and are less likely to grow and accept their full responsibility.

As a CEO, I must manage risk, but I cannot eliminate it. Endeavors to eliminate risk strangle and stunt relationships rather than giving them space to breath and grow. Our authors speak of scientific management, an approach that believes it can eliminate any risk. But by trying to eliminate all risk, this approach alienates the human person, destroys creativity and autonomy, and even threatens life itself—because life by its delightful, mysterious nature is fraught with risk. Business without risk is the antithesis of business. Rigidly risk-averse business leaders seek to rationalize their decisions so much so that they often handicap themselves with delay, and this can result in the instrumentalization of employees who are forced to act on a decision made too late.

Risk is the essence of trust, and instrumentalization is its absolute negation.

⁞ ⁞ ⁞

As Christians we know the unimaginable freedom that we have been granted as human persons through the unlimited love of our Creator. True freedom can only be granted by the truest, greatest love. God chose in his infinite goodness to give us the ultimate freedom to accept or reject his love and certainly, as Passion Week reminds us so vividly every year, we have too often abused this gift. In full subsidiarity, however, God teaches us something about how we might make better use of our free will to build up a civilization of love and his eternal Kingdom. He has sent us numerous teachers along the way—prophets to chasten us, martyrs to inspire us, saints to exhort us, and families to form and love us, and to show us just how great his love is—a love so great it would not withhold any gift, even his most beloved Son.

There is no overbearing "top-down" approach to the management of heaven; God will never instrumentalize his creation. In God's perfect design, we have been created with free will, and in return he freely accepts all of the risk associated with it on our behalf. This freedom is at the root of our humanity and of our ability to love and to respond to his love. It is the foundation of our ability to pursue co-creation with the Creator. What a generous and wonderful lesson in holy management.

Risk is indeed at the root of our humanity—and at the root of subsidiarity. I hope this essay will help all its readers to enter into the extraordinary paradox that the risk deliberately accepted, combined with a deep-rooted solidarity, is the key to a management approach that will offer to all workers the possibility of integral human development while delivering a superior efficiency in creating valuable goods and services. For Christians, this is the very definition of *good work*.

My sincere congratulations and deep thanks to the University of St. Thomas, and in particular to the John A. Ryan and Veritas Institutes who led us through this journey. My dream is that this essay will be useful for the UNIAPAC associations, universities, and businesses that see management and leadership as creating highly efficient and profitable companies ordered to the development of employees who will joyfully serve the world.

Pierre Lecocq
UNIAPAC President, 2009–2013
Inergy Automotive Systems S.A., CEO, 2002–2015
Paris, January 2015

INTRODUCTION

How I wish everyone had decent work! It is essential for human dignity.
POPE FRANCIS[1]

We must as leaders embrace the principle of subsidiarity. It is wrong to steal
a person's right or ability to make a decision. If we do so, it will ultimately
cripple the firm, with people caught up in activities to please their boss rather than to satisfy the customer. Delegation and decision-making at the point
closest to the customer are imperative. Delegation without a framework of
authority, however, will result in chaos.
WILLIAM POLLARD, former CEO of *ServiceMaster*[2]

1. **WHEN WE SEE THE TERM "STEALING,"** we usually think of the loss of things, money, or property. William Pollard, however, speaks of stealing people's decision-making abilities, and by extension their skills or gifts. Theft of any kind is an injustice, but stealing people's decisions and gifts robs them of an essential part of their humanity—their ability to give their best selves to others in the work they do. It also effectively robs the organization by limiting the value of an employee's contribution. An organization can only reach its full potential for excellence when its workers are also given the opportunity to reach their full potential. As Pollard points out, however, while subsidiarity should foster employees' gifts through work, it does so within a framework of authority and accountability. This creates a natural tension, one that we will address throughout this essay.

2. Our purpose is to examine the principle of subsidiarity in the context of organizational leadership. The word "subsidiarity" comes from the Latin *subsidium*, that is, "to assist or strengthen" the other. Within organizations, subsidiarity serves as a moral principle that directs leaders to place decision-making at the most appropriate level of an organization so as to utilize the gifts of employees for their own good, the good of the organization, and the good of the organization's clients or customers. In practice it serves several important ends: it helps employees develop through their work; it builds trust among leaders and subordinates; and it strengthens the identity and culture of a firm.

3.   Subsidiarity is based on the understanding that each person has a right to be respected, and that each person bears gifts to be exercised. Leaders are at their best, according to this principle, when they build organizations that actively draw upon the diverse gifts (talents, abilities, and skills) of all employees. Creating conditions where these gifts can flourish is the most authentic approach to employee development. These conditions also provide the basis for a morally good and productive company. The lens of giftedness allows leaders to see employees as persons who have much to give and gain within a community of work, and not merely as capital to be exploited or resources to be used. Subsidiarity provides a key for understanding what "good work" really is.[3] It challenges business leaders to imagine what might be possible if the potential of all the human gifts within their organizations were fully realized. Resting on a *logic of gift* and complemented by the principle of solidarity, subsidiarity sees in each person "a subject who is always capable of giving something to others."[4]

4.   Management literature, while using different language, echoes the themes of subsidiarity. Peter Drucker described this lens of giftedness in terms of "making strengths productive," and identified this as a fundamental way both to respect the person and to build up an organization. "In making strengths productive, the executive integrates individual purpose and organization needs, individual capacity and organization results, individual achievement and organization opportunity."[5] As Drucker's reflection emphasizes, respect for the person is a cornerstone for the effectiveness of the organization, its executives, and its employees. Charles A. O'Reilly and Jeffrey Pfeffer espouse similar views when they speak about leaders and their companies unlocking "the hidden value in all their employees."[6]

5. Unfortunately, the history of institutions and earlier managerial writings based on a mechanistic view of labor reveal a tendency toward micromanagement, excessive centralization of authority, and treating employees as mere means—all of which stifle the expression of individual gifts, talents, and skills. Such practices limit the growth and expression of the overall human capacity in the organization and they disengage employees as well. Navigating through turbulent waters tempts leaders to tighten controls by creating more rules and oversight mechanisms.[7] When tighter controls become routine, however, they can rob employees of initiative, creativity, and responsibility. Asking only the minimum of employees and denying them the opportunity to contribute more fully not only wastes their natural gifts, but insults their dignity.[8] This is the stuff of ethically troubled institutions, and, ironically, inefficient ones as well.

6. Subsidiarity in action—appreciating the collective gifts of employees and putting those gifts to work—requires psychological connectedness, spiritual maturity, and the virtue of trust. It calls upon leaders to embrace a vision that is larger than the calculus of personal advancement. Subsidiarity is not simply a technique for prompting people to work harder, though it will in most cases create more efficient and productive institutions. It is first and foremost a moral principle, supporting a management philosophy that respects persons and allows them to contribute and flourish in the workplace. It asks managers to look at the gifts present among their employees, and having seen them, to act, creating conditions that allow further discovery and the exercise of those gifts through work. Trusted to use their gifts, employees are likely to reciprocate with increased trust of leadership. Where trust is high, efficiency, too, can thrive, along with personal dignity and satisfaction.

7. Subsidiarity requires a mindful approach to organizational elements—job design, training and development, decision-making processes, hierarchy, and delegated authority—allowing persons and groups to develop and effectively use their talents, skills, and abilities. To achieve these ends, some decisions may need to be relocated—to higher or lower levels, or laterally within the organization. Greater autonomy may be necessary in certain cases and centralization or standardization in others. In some circumstances subsidiarity may suggest shared authority, in others, unilateral authority.[9] There are no simple formulae for enacting subsidiarity; good judgment on what may be required depends on the leader's ability to assess the unique features of a situation. Trust, too, is key. For leaders to exercise their judgment while remaining engaged with employees requires sufficient trust among all parties. Without trust in their leaders, employees may well question motives for increasing or decreasing degrees of decision-making. Similarly, for leaders to make such changes in the first place implicitly requires trust in the employees who will make those changes work.[10]

8. The leadership challenge of subsidiarity involves a three-stage process: *seeing* situations clearly; *judging* with principles that foster the integral development of people; and *acting* in a way that implements these principles in light of the unique circumstances at hand.[11] We have organized the reflections that follow around these three stages.

9. *Seeing,* in the present context, means more than just looking and grasping details, or analyzing a situation or set of facts in some value-free, detached, or antiseptic fashion. It means looking intentionally, employing reason and empathy to understand the whole. *Acting* includes a broad range of familiar management and leadership tasks, from seeking counsel and input, to deciding, planning, implementing, adjusting, and measuring outcomes. Like seeing, acting is not merely the result of some mechanical formula; it is informed by the intention to increase the good, both for the organization and for the person.

10. For some, however, *judging* may be the most problematic concept in our three-fold structure. In this postmodern age, using terms like "judging" or "moral judgment" often elicits resistance. One business leader in private conversation with the authors remarked, "Statements about morally good management or morally bad management should be avoided because they turn executives off." The causes of such negative reactions range from uneasiness at the idea of being ethically "judgmental," to outright disapproval of "moral assertiveness" as a kind of imperialism. Such resistance, we believe, is misguided, for it confuses two different ideas, "judging" and "being judgmental," at the cost of abdicating responsibility for using our minds to form well-reasoned judgments about the moral quality of behavior—our own and others. This is a duty we all share.

11. Oxford philosopher Mary Midgley explains the vital, productive role of moral judgment for the development of people and cultures:

> The power of moral judgement is, in fact, *not* a luxury, *not* a perverse indulgence of the self-righteous. *It is a necessity.* When we judge something to be bad or good, better or worse than something else, we are taking it as an example to aim at or avoid. Without opinions of this sort, we would have no framework of comparison for our own policy, no chance

of profiting by other people's insights or mistakes. In this vacuum, we could form no judgements on *our own* actions. (Emphasis added.)[12]

Being judgmental, on the other hand, stands in contrast to the moral judgment that Midgley so eloquently defends. Being judgmental is the trait of being arrogant or disparaging of individuals or groups—of "rushing to judgment"[13] on the basis of very limited or poor evidence. This, of course, leads to misjudgment, or crude judgments, which prudent leaders must avoid.

12. When normative judgments (judgments employing "shoulds" and "oughts," "rights" and "wrongs," "good, better, and best") are not made explicit and defended with thoughtful reasons, they do not simply disappear. Rather, they go "underground" as unaccountable assumptions in discussions and decisions about which pathways individuals and organizations should take. When business leaders make moral judgments, as they inevitably do, reliance on principles grounded in a correct understanding of the human person is an indispensable aid in explaining and defending those judgments.[14] Subsidiarity is one such principle. At the heart of "subsidiarity leadership" is a *respect in action* that assists leaders to take another look (*re-spect* from the Latin *respectare* to re-look) at their employees. This *relooking* calls leaders to move beyond first impressions, and to recognize the unrepeatable, irreplaceable personal reality of each employee. For leaders this "relooking" helps to build organizations that actively draw upon the diverse gifts, talents, abilities, and skills of all employees.

CHAPTER 1

SEEING
Subsidiarity Today and Yesterday

13. **THE CHALLENGE OF CREATING JOBS** is paramount in nearly every economy. But the challenge of creating *good work* is also with us. Whereas the former task is the mother of the latter, the latter addresses the quality and effectiveness of these jobs. In our view, subsidiarity is a necessary principle for the creation of good work. There are forces at play within the modern corporation that make it difficult to operationalize this principle. Yet none of these dampen our conviction that abundant opportunities to exercise subsidiarity exist and that we act wisely in taking the time to *see* them. In this chapter, we will explore both the contemporary obstacles and opportunities of operationalizing subsidiarity as well as the historical context from which this principle derives.

Obstacles and Opportunities

14. One indicator of good work is that people are engaged in their jobs. The rate of employee engagement (vs. non-engagement or active disengagement) among world-class companies may be as high as two-thirds of their workforce. Organizations with engaged employees outperform those with disengaged employees as measured by lower employee turnover, less absenteeism, fewer safety accidents, higher

Workforce Disengagement in the US

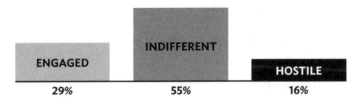

ENGAGED	INDIFFERENT	HOSTILE
29%	55%	16%

employee satisfaction, faster growth, healthier margins, better customer relations, and fewer quality defects.[15]

15. Studies among non-world-class companies indicate that as many as 70 percent of employees are indifferent or hostile to their work. Reporting on one such US study, "State of the American Workplace: Employee Engagement Insights for U.S. Business Leaders," Gallup estimated that the impact of employee disengagement costs American businesses $450–550 billion annually. Workers who are disengaged "are not reaching their full potential," says the Gallup report. The good news in the report is "that managers who focus on their employees' strengths can practically eliminate active disengagement" and double the level of engagement of workers.[16] The principle of subsidiarity, focused as it is on appreciating the gifts of employees and putting those gifts to work, opens a way for leaders to avoid the dysfunctional climate and negative business outcomes produced by excessive control and the waste of human potential.

16. There are many reasons for disengagement. Corporate systems and structures frequently discourage important expressions of subsidiarity like cooperation and shared problem solving. Compensation practices can also contribute to disengagement. On one end of the spectrum are performance standards stressing individual achievement that can generate dysfunctional competition among executives and among employees throughout the organization. "Winning the competition" also contributes to the extreme pay differentials that seem to separate top managers from everyone else. On the other end of the spectrum are labor agreements that reflect neither the concept of subsidiarity nor its spirit. Instead the focus seems to be on delineating roles and responsibilities in a rigid manner, reinforcing a mechanical vision of the organization's operations and each employee's role. None of these practices readily support cultures, systems, or practices necessary for subsidiarity to flourish. Where good communication, cooperation, and shared commitment are in short supply, subsidiarity is made difficult, if not impossible. Excessive specialization and an unwillingness to question processes and procedures do not make a welcoming environment for subsidiarity. More broadly, the pressures of public stock ownership and attendant governance structures that emphasize short-run concerns may unduly limit the freedom of managers to discern paths to more effective long-run benefits. Job losses, layoffs, and a preference for part-time or lower paying positions also contribute to disengagement. In such circumstances, subsidiarity may be seen as too risky to be tried.

17. Among the challenges to a culture of subsidiarity are increasing financial and competitive pressures in the global economy. Where labor costs are seen as key to competing effectively, corporate leaders naturally try to reduce these costs, either by lowering wage rates or by enhancing productivity.[17] When cost pressures are extreme, designing more dignified jobs and taking time to listen to employees can seem to be peripheral concerns, if not distractions from the real work at hand. Job design is further complicated by the fast pace of business. Changes in staffing, structure, and goals occur rapidly and repeatedly as firms try to adapt to shifts in critical markets or industries. Communication technologies support the pace of business and sometimes drive it. They, too, affect workplace relationships, by making virtual meetings and long-distance supervision possible, by increasing pressure to be available twenty-four hours a day, seven days a week, if needed, and by eliminating the real-time, face-to-face human interaction that is essential to building trust.

18. Unfortunately, some leaders react to economic and competitive pressures with limited attention to their moral and spiritual dimensions. Solutions that instrumentalize workers, frenetic and unrelenting work schedules, and diminished long-term vision for the sake of meeting quarterly goals—these are but a few of the business practices laden with moral issues. Furthermore, proceduralism, bureaucratic rule, and a reflexive dependence on "what our policy requires" may substitute for sound employee judgment.

19. A very public and tragic example of this pattern was the January 28, 1986, loss of the Space Shuttle *Challenger*, which has been the subject of multiple studies for more than 20 years. There is reason to believe that the decision to launch the *Challenger* was embedded in a bureaucratic culture focused on achieving promised goals and pleasing politicians—a culture with a "history of grandiose promises, funding shortfalls, political handicaps, and technical compromises."[18] In crises or under excessive pressure, leaders are tempted to rely too much on co-ercive authority to dominate decision-making and to impose solutions. In the words of one successful entrepreneur, "Authoritarians cannot impose commitments, only commands."[19] Commands may be followed, but the leader who relies on them risks mistaking employee compliance for true acceptance of the leader's goals or vision.

20. Organizational cultures like these are almost certain to end in employee disengagement or disconnection. Decisions that depersonalize workers and fail to respect their humanity put the organization at risk. Damage to mutual trust may linger in the workplace for a very long time, affecting attitudes, commitment, relationships, and, of course, organizational performance.

21. Obstacles to subsidiarity, however, are not the whole story. Many businesses have adopted managerial approaches that support subsidiarity. The Total Quality Management (TQM) movement serves as one such example.[20] TQM challenged the prevailing management practice of "inspecting in" quality on the assumption that superior knowledge of products and processes lay with management experts. "Bureaucratic" rigidity and role distinctions were not the road to continuous quality improvement or manufacturing success. TQM systematized methods for harnessing the talents of knowledgeable workers to make continuous quality improvements. It did this by driving out fear—and by creating conditions to utilize the full talents and contributions of employees.

22. The advantages of subsidiarity have become increasingly evident with the emergence of the Internet during the past several decades. In a digital age, it is nearly impossible for any single group of knowledge workers to claim a monopoly on information or on methods. Overwhelming amounts of information move too freely and too rapidly to be managed by centralization and formalization. For many organizations, corporate strategy has become flexible, changeable, and subject to continuous adjustment. In an economy where the distribution of knowledge is increasingly broad, employees throughout the organization possess critical elements of this knowledge. If these individuals become disaffected, a company becomes incapable of responding successfully to the fast-changing environment.[21] Many companies today give business units the freedom to engage in rapid, cross-functional communications unhampered by bureaucratic impediments. Close ties to differentiated market segments, for example, allow quick and easy adaptation to customers' changing needs. Units often conduct product or service testing in partnership with customers, yielding insights that can improve and refine new offerings *before* they come to market. Accountability for innovation, quality, market response, and financial performance also rests with the units. These new approaches are built on the ideas of distributed information and distributed authority, concepts close to the spirit of subsidiarity.[22]

23.   Intel offers an early example of the impact of diffused knowledge on corporate strategy in a fast-paced industry. An article in the *Harvard Business Review* described former CEO Andy Grove's acknowledgement that

> for a long time neither he nor other top Intel executives were willing or able to see how the competitive environment had undermined the company's strategy of being a major player in both memory chips and microprocessors. Yet for two full years before top management woke up to this reality, various project leaders, marketing managers, and plant supervisors were busy refocusing Intel's strategy by shifting resources from memories to microprocessors. Management, Grove confessed, might have been "fooled by our strategic rhetoric, but those on the front lines could see that we had to retreat from memory chips. . . . People formulate strategy with their fingertips. Our most significant strategic decision was made not in response to some clear-sighted corporate vision but by the marketing and investment decisions of frontline managers who really knew what was going on.[23]

24.   To capitalize on this insight, organizations are wise to foster initiative—to develop engaged employees. When initiative is incorporated into the design of work—especially day-to-day work—employees are given a voice. This voice lays the groundwork for innovation, creativity, and a sense of shared responsibility or ownership. Gaining the advantages of fostering this voice requires leaders to encourage collaboration, decentralization, and accountability. Employee initiative, when broadly nurtured, can put a powerful collective intelligence at the service of the whole organization, an intelligence greater than any centralized management system can deliver.[24]

25. Fostering initiative, of course, can also reveal tensions and disagreements. Difficult conversations are inevitable. The way forward may not be clear or universally acknowledged. But if managed well, candid and even difficult discussions, in which unwelcome information is allowed to surface, can enhance the decision process. With many voices, knowledge takes precedence over power, privilege, or group loyalty. Decisions made through participative processes are usually *better decisions* because they are based on more information and less bias, and because the inclusive process itself generates acceptance. Though it takes time and resources, employee participation helps an organization avoid the costs of failing to anticipate key elements, and the costs associated with resistance. Leaders who take the time to look, and to *see* the dynamics in contemporary business, will recognize both opportunities and obstacles to pursuing a culture of subsidiarity.

26. Management scholar Domènec Melé describes how Fremap, a Spanish non-profit mutual insurance company, evolved from its overly-rigid bureaucratic structure to a more flexible one in which job designs could connect with a human dimension (i.e., create meaningful work). Under the former management structure, Melé notes, insurance paperwork would move through as many as eight employees who each addressed only single parts of a claim. With subsidiarity in place, for the most part, one person could manage the entire claim. Employees became motivated. Quality improved. Customers were satisfied. Fremap flourished.[25]

27. Clearly, there is a business case for subsidiarity, but to see this as the only or even the principal reason for its practice is to understate its moral importance. Subsidiarity goes beyond arguments based on economic performance and organizational excellence. An authentic adoption of the principle of subsidiarity in the workplace requires a correct understanding of the human person.[26] In our view, a true commitment to subsidiarity rests on a managerial perspective that sees the person as central in relation to the enterprise. To develop that perspective, leaders may require formation beyond graduate degrees and leadership training, formation that begins with an understanding of the spiritual and moral roots of subsidiarity. (See Chapter 2)

Historical Connections

28. While seeing subsidiarity in relation to current situations is essential, understanding the principle in a historical context can awaken business leaders to the challenge and calling to humanize work environments. The idea of subsidiarity has been in evidence in Western political thought for centuries. In the twentieth century, the principle can be found in the language of the Maastricht Treaty forming the European Union (1992), the various reports of the United Nations Human Development Program, and the European Union's Charter of Fundamental Rights (2000). It is evident in modern governmental structures as well. The federal system established by the US Constitution displays clear affinities with subsidiarity. But the principle is older still. Its roots can be traced to ancient Rome: "In the Latin vocabulary the word *subsidium* initially meant something in reserve or, more specifically, reserve troops: troops used in the case of necessity. The expression 'subsidium ferre' means to stay behind and be prepared to help those who find themselves in trouble on the front line."[27]

29. The core meaning of subsidiarity, therefore, is "to assist," or to strengthen, to stand behind or beneath. A higher authority or social body can assist a lower (or subsidiary) body in two ways. The first is more passive: higher authority does not absorb or supplant the initiative of a lower body on issues where the latter should exercise freedom and initiative. The second way is proactive: higher authority helps a lower body where the latter is unable to accomplish an essential task on its own. Subsidiarity, therefore, calls for higher authority to provide help in a way that fosters not dependence, but "freedom and participation through assumption of responsibility."[28]

30. Subsidiarity emerged explicitly as a formal principle within Catholic social teaching during the 1930s, when totalitarian regimes rose to power in the West. Communism, fascism, and Nazism all sought to absorb within the state the responsibilities of families, schools, churches, and voluntary groups. Lacking vibrant, intermediary bodies, life in the societies ruled by these regimes was dominated by the individual's relationship with the nation state. Pope Pius XI promulgated the encyclical *Quadragesimo Anno* in 1931, largely to protest this development. There he described subsidiarity as a "principle of social philosophy."

31. The principle of subsidiarity, Pius emphasized, protects intermediate associations (the family, business, religion, education, and volunteers) from the unjustified loss of authority and freedom that results when power is concentrated excessively within the state.[29] Subsidiarity directs higher-level social entities, such as the state, to support rather than usurp the activities and responsibilities of more basic social institutions and associations.

32. Although initially used with reference to government, the principle of subsidiarity applies to virtually any institution, including business.[30] Early efforts to develop thinking about subsidiarity within Church teaching were made at a time when industrial corporations were experiencing extraordinary growth in scope and power. Managers exercised significant control over workers as a consequence of several factors: the de-skilling of jobs that resulted from the division of labor, increased power among capital holders, and government passivity in economic affairs. Centralized corporate bureaucracies designed production systems and jobs to serve efficiency above all else.

33. Within these systems, the good of workers, while not ignored altogether, was an afterthought. Many laborers, absorbed in strenuous, monotonous, and often dangerous work for twelve or more hours each day, experienced industrial employment as a great burden—an alienating drudgery that harmed their health, curtailed social interaction, and separated them from family, from nature, and from the value of their labor.

34. In *The Wealth of Nations*, Adam Smith noted that the pursuit of a division of labor could impede the intellectual, social, and physical development of workers. With their employment reduced to "a few simple operations," Smith warned that workers would lose the habit of applying their mind and understanding: They would become "incapable of rational conversation" and "of conceiving any generous, noble, or tender sentiment, and consequently of forming any just judgment concerning many even of the ordinary duties of private life."[31]

35. Roughly sixty years later, the French political philosopher Alexis de Tocqueville echoed Smith's concerns. Observing industrial operations in the United States during the early 1830s, Tocqueville noted how the production of goods was subdivided into specialized subtasks. He commented upon the implications of this approach for the worker:

When a workman is constantly and exclusively engaged in making one object, he ends by performing this work with singular dexterity. But at the same time, he loses the general faculty of applying his mind to the way he is working. Every day he becomes more adroit and less industrious, and one may say that in his case the man is degraded as the workman improves. [...] As the principle of the division of labor is ever more completely applied, the workman becomes weaker, more limited, and more dependent. The craft improves, the craftsman slips back.[32]

36. Later in the nineteenth century, Karl Marx decried the alienation he saw emerging from the industrial workplace of his day. Insofar as owners controlled the design and production of goods, and owners received most of the monetary value generated from the sale of these goods, Marx viewed workers as profoundly alienated from the fruits of their labor, the products they helped to create. Performing jobs comprised of endlessly recurring movements, the work process dehumanized members of the workforce: They were reduced to mere "cogs in a machine." Marx contended that owners' desire for ever-higher returns would push wages downward to subsistence levels and would trap workers within a brutish, hand-to-mouth existence.

37. One significant movement in the early twentieth century advanced operational efficiency at the expense of subsidiarity within corporations—Frederick Winslow Taylor's "scientific management."[33] Taylor's studies of manufacturing and the steel industry were motivated in part by a desire to better understand inefficient and frequently dangerous production processes. To do this, Taylor used empirical techniques. His dispassionate observation, record-keeping, and comparisons did much to enhance operational efficiency and improve worker safety. Ultimately, his research gave rise to the discipline of time and motion analysis, which radically transformed industrial operations. In an era when work days, bookkeeping, training, tools, work methods, and quality were not standardized, business leaders welcomed Taylor's conviction that there was "one best way" to manage in any given situation.

38. While improving productivity and profits was Taylor's primary goal, he also sought to use scientific management to enhance workers' wellbeing. But his engineering background led him to see industrial processes as analogous to mechanical systems. Consequently, he viewed workers primarily as components within a broader production system. In his ideal industrial world, managers would dictate the terms of the work to employees: "The managers assume . . . the burden of gathering together all of the traditional knowledge which in the past has been possessed by the workmen and then of classifying, tabulating, and reducing this knowledge to rules, laws, and formulae."[34]

39. Taylor was both lauded and condemned for his research. The founders of the MBA program at Harvard University were so influenced by his thinking that they invited Taylor to lecture annually at their school. The US Congress, on the other hand, investigated him on accusations that he was "dehumanizing" work. Joseph Stalin used Taylor's principles to justify the USSR's disastrous economic system; and adaptations of Taylor's scientific methods and Henry Ford's manufacturing methods were evident in both the thinking and initiatives of Hitler and Mussolini. In the Depression-era movie, *Modern Times* (1936), Charlie Chaplin's "Little Tramp" struggled to survive in a cold and cruel industrial setting awash in the symbols and products of scientific management. In light of the trend toward detailed managerial control, many expressed concern about the increasing depersonalization of work.[35]

40. During the same period, voices in the Christian social tradition expressed concern about this depersonalization. Pius XI highlighted the moral contradictions of an industrialization that everywhere reduced human labor "to an instrument of strange perversion: *for dead matter leaves the factory ennobled and transformed, while men are corrupted and degraded.*"[36] Rather than shaping the organization to the nature of the person, corporations tended to conform themselves to the demands of capital, and to a completely technocratic structure. A production process that removes decision making from the worker and reduces work to a "series of identical movements . . . threatens to take away from work any hint of humanity, making of it a merely mechanical activity."[37]

41. The warnings voiced by Adam Smith, Alexis de Tocqueville, and Karl Marx about repetitive, "mind-deadening," alienating work deserve serious management attention. Some would argue that in every age, menial agricultural work or assembly line work is *inherently* depersonalizing—even dehumanizing—while still being necessary.[38] In such contexts, respectfully using the gifts of workers may have to take innovative forms, such as (a) limiting the time intervals expected of workers while assuring that wage compensation is just; (b) engaging workers themselves in improving the work process or other working conditions; (c) automating the work in question while training workers to make higher-level contributions; and (d) guarding against growing demands on worker productivity in relation to the private lives of employees. Human dignity is affected not only by considerations of work life *quality* but also by encroachment upon the amount of time available outside of work for a balanced life.

42. When properly understood and applied to organizations, the principle of subsidiarity serves as a guide to avoid these injustices within corporations. We now turn our attention to understanding this principle as a criterion of judgment.

CHAPTER 2

JUDGING
The Moral and Spiritual Roots of Subsidiarity

43. **ALL MANAGERS HAVE VALUE-LADEN VIEWS OF WORK.** This simple but important insight becomes clear in examining both the current situation and the history of business and organizational life. There simply is no value-free stance on work's purpose and meaning. Even when leaders do not articulate them, their values reveal themselves in daily decisions and strategic choices with significant implications for others. Furthermore, financial pressures and individualistic tendencies may cause leaders unwittingly to displace justice with expediency, wisdom with power, and the common good with personal or organizational self-interest.[39] When business leaders do not embrace the deep moral and spiritual roots underlying subsidiarity, they risk reducing subsidiarity and other principles like it to mere management techniques that result in exchanges between leaders and employees that are entirely instrumental, even dehumanizing. In this chapter, we confront the prevailing business temptation to instrumentalism and explore the deep roots of subsidiarity found within the "logic of gift" as well as the complementary principle of solidarity.

The Challenge of Instrumentalism

44. As a guide to judgment about what constitutes good work, the principle of subsidiarity has two important goals: one is moral; the other, as discussed in the previous chapter, is economic. The moral goal is to build up an organization in which initiative is fostered, talents and skills are exercised and developed, relationships are strong, and trust is deep. The economic goal is to make the organization competitive in the marketplace by providing excellent and usable products and services that generate sufficient profit to sustain the business. Both the "ought" of the moral principle and the "can" of economic and technical competence are needed.

45. At its best, subsidiarity fosters a "coentrepreneurial" culture that helps the organization respond to the marketplace, operate effectively and, in general, become a good place to work.[40] Subsidiarity, when correctly understood and applied, enhances the organization both morally (by creating trusting relationships) and economically (by improving efficiency and effectiveness). When leaders tap employee creativity, initiative, and innovation to create "goods that are *truly* good and services that *truly* serve,"[41] they develop deeper relationships with their employees. In most cases, subsidiarity yields greater effectiveness because it yields better goods, services, and methods, and greater efficiency and healthier margins because people are operating at their best.

46. As suggested in the previous section, subsidiarity can be practiced merely for its potential to enhance efficiency and profitability. This is attractive, because it suggests that the economic logic of business (profitability) is served by the moral logic of corporate conscience or business responsibility. Yet, it is subversive because it treats moral expectations as if they had no independent validity for business decision makers. The limitation of this line of instrumental rationality is captured well by Lynn Paine of Harvard Business School when she writes:

> Ethics has gained legitimacy among corporate executives principally by proving its economic value. However, embedded in the confident assertion that "ethics pays" is a nagging question: "What if it didn't?" Suppose that a company could earn supernormal returns for a reasonable period of time through methods such as using suppliers who rely on bonded child workers, spreading false rumors about its competitors, concealing product hazards from customers, betraying its contracts, polluting the water supply, or undermining the social fabric. Are ethical reservations therefore to be set aside and these methods recommended? [42]

The point here is that if we limit conscience (moral responsibility) to fit the economic logic of individual or corporate self-interest, we weaken our ability to question the logic of the market, except perhaps in terms of the time horizon involved (i.e., "long-term" vs. "short-term"). Even more importantly, an instrumental logic by itself depersonalizes the relationship between leaders and employees. Without social, moral, and spiritual underpinnings, subsidiarity loses its power to humanize organizations: it becomes just one more way to instrumentalize employees, who rarely miss this point. For example, the progress of the TQM movement has been hindered by executives who have used its techniques as just another way to "right-size" organizations through layoffs. To paraphrase T. S. Eliot, it is "to do the right deed for the wrong reason," which is "the greatest treason."[43] To act well, leaders must first see well and judge well; to judge well they must intend well. Only then will they earn the trust of their employees.[44] To judge the efficacy of subsidiarity one must see it in its fullness—roots and all. Leaders who are authentically drawn to subsidiarity see the implications of recognizing the gifts of individual persons. Creating the conditions within the organization that allow these gifts to develop and flourish honors human dignity.

47. A spiritual and moral root system may help business leaders avoid the problem of instrumentalism just described. Without such grounding, there is the risk of drifting during difficult times.[45] It is not easy to achieve common agreement on principles and their roots. But disagreement itself is nothing to fear and is certainly no reason to stop seeking consensus. Understanding the basis for our beliefs about how humans should behave toward one another is an essential step in validating and affirming them. What is true for other principles is also true for subsidiarity. So we ask, where does this idea come from?

The Logic of Gift

48. **The Giftedness of Persons.** The most basic framework underlying subsidiarity is the *logic of gift*.[46] It flows from the idea that humans have gifts—talents, skills, and special abilities—that may be shared for the good of all.[47] One of the deepest implications of the logic of gift is that we can only fully discover ourselves through sharing our gifts with others. We make ourselves a self-gift.[48] It follows that such gifts should not be commoditized or exploited, and that they are not to be wasted or taken for granted. Subsidiarity, by this logic, does not seek to drive people to excel but to *free* them to develop their talents, skills, and knowledge, and to share these gifts with others for a greater good.[49] We do not grow as persons by claiming autonomy or by pursuing self-interest; a life of self-centeredness only makes us lonely. Rather, we grow through relationships, through bonds of communion, when our gifts move through us in service to others.[50] The business leader's responsibility, then, is to recognize these gifts—their kind and multiplicity. Creating an organizational culture for developing and cultivating those gifts is a significant challenge. Between seeing and acting lies *judgment*, prudential judgment, or practical wisdom, which is perhaps the central virtue for all leaders. Practical wisdom takes its bearings from the good; that is, it understands what the good is and seeks the good not only for the one judging but for others, too. In business, such wisdom follows from the recognition that all members of the firm—executives, administrative assistants, janitors, engineers, and all workers—have gifts and an inherent human dignity. Consequently, they never should be treated as only resources or mere instruments of production, but as persons for whom (and by whom) the good must be sought.

49. **The Gift Giver.** While the root system focuses on the gifted nature of the person, it raises the obvious spiritual and religious question: *Where do the gifts come from?* This question sits uncomfortably in current secular Western culture. More and more, religious and spiritual questions are seen as marginal, unhelpful, and even dangerous within the public sphere. This trend is regrettable. In the words of Vaclav Havel, the ideals of human society (which include subsidiarity, human rights, and human dignity), "will mean nothing as long as [these imperatives do] not derive from the respect for the miracle of Being, the miracle of the universe, the miracle of nature, the miracle of our own existence."[51] Havel clearly points to the need for a spiritual root system to ground our ideals. Cultural institutions such as the family, religion, and education need to be part of the discussion because it is their moral and spiritual logic that forms business leaders.

50. By emphasizing subsidiarity's root system we do not mean to shortchange its basis in human reason. Our point is a broader one. That is, when separated from a larger transcendent reality, reason is eventually reduced to its instrumental characteristics. When faith and transcendence are cut off from reason, they move toward superstition and fundamentalism, undermining a healthy spiritual path. On the other hand, when reason is cut off from faith and transcendence, it leads toward a dictatorship of efficiency, toward the dominance of instrumentalism, and ultimately to a lack of community.[52] This is especially true in business: the logic of the market, which defines value strictly in terms of profit, productivity, and acquisitions, is always seeking ascendency. Subsidiarity is best understood, therefore, as both rational and connected to a transcendent reality. Below we describe a monotheistic root system that gives life to subsidiarity.

51. The responsibility to create conditions in which employees' gifts can be exercised is *rooted* in God's creative act. This is revealed in the first chapters of Genesis: that all people possess dignity because they are *imago Dei*—made in the image and likeness of God. The tradition teaches that though we are not God, God's creation is reflected in our human capacities. Christianity, in particular, holds that precisely because we are made in God's image, our work should participate in "the very action of the Creator of the universe."[53] In other words, God's creation is not a one-time event, but an unfolding activity in which we are called to participate, to respond to God's command to exercise dominion. Dominion is not a license for exploitation. Rather, it requires the responsible employment of the gifts we have been given, our talents and capabilities, to make the world a better place. In this light, work is fundamentally a participation in the ongoing process of creation.

52. In the final analysis, therefore, creation itself is our model for subsidiarity. It is a revealed truth about creation that "God has not willed to reserve to himself all exercise of power."[54] Instead, God has entrusted certain gifts and roles to each creature. For human persons, these gifts are central to understanding their mission and vocation. Gifts endow us with the capacity to act not simply for ourselves. Our gifts are meant to go *through us to others*.[55] Exercising our capacity for self-gift—that is, sharing our talents, abilities, and skills—is one of the fundamental ways in which each human person manifests the *imago Dei*.

53.   In entrusting us with certain capacities or gifts, God has given us freedom and intelligence. We flourish as human beings when we make the best use of our freedom and intelligence. This truth is the basis for the judgment that human dignity is diminished when freedom and intelligence are unnecessarily constrained or suppressed in business organizations or elsewhere. When they embrace subsidiarity, leaders acknowledge that there are risks associated with inviting people to use their gifts and their own judgment. Accepting the risk inherent in trusting others, leaders affirm that the freedom and intelligence of employees should never be suppressed or disregarded.

54.   We should not, however, mistake freedom for license to do whatever one wants. This path can lead to chaos. As D. H. Lawrence wisely observed, once you are able to do whatever you want, "there is nothing you care about doing."[56] Freedom is not the arbitrary will of personal preference. True and intelligent freedom lies in doing what we *need* to do, what we are *created* to do—not simply what we *want* to do. Freedom that acts without truth disorders judgment: a counterfeit, it leads not to liberation, but to enslavement, social fragmentation, and ultimately injustice.[57]

The Principle of Solidarity

55.   Despite the importance and dynamic quality of subsidiarity, neither it nor any other single principle can fully articulate good business leadership. This is why in the Catholic social tradition, subsidiarity is regularly complemented with another principle, *solidarity*, or unity for a common good. Solidarity helps to fulfill subsidiarity and prevent potential distortions.[58] Where the "logic of gift" gives subsidiarity roots, the principle of solidarity complements subsidiarity by providing a more complete vision of good work.

56. We find that every principle and idea, in order to be realized, needs a complement, without which it would fade. As we mentioned above, freedom and truth are interdependent: without truth, freedom becomes license; without freedom, truth degenerates into authoritarianism. Rights and duties are also inextricably linked: without duties, which link us in community, rights spawn selfish individualism; without rights affirming human dignity, duties collapse into blind obedience and rule-following rigidity.

57. Similarly, subsidiarity and solidarity can be distorted. Benedict XVI captured this difficulty by pointing out that when subsidiarity loses sight of solidarity it "gives way to social privatism."[59] When leaders create a workplace where the diversity of talents is exercised (subsidiarity), but closed to solidarity, they risk fostering attitudes that are increasingly self-referential and employees who are isolated from the market and the larger community. The unintended consequence may be a culture of entitlement. In such a culture, employees focus more on their rights and less on their duties and responsibilities to the whole. An increasing amount of time might be devoted to internal debates and problems within the organization, such as working conditions, autonomy, pay, benefits, and work rules. Such single-minded thinking can become a fixation; it can lead an organization to overlook the importance of hiring for mission and forming a shared identity.

58. Solidarity can be thought of as a compass, orienting subsidiarity (the cultivation of individual talents and responsibilities) toward the common good, preventing undisciplined empowerment. People want to be connected to something bigger than themselves. They "need a sense of moral authority, derived not from a focus on the efficiency of means but from the importance of the ends they produce."[60]

59. Conversely, when solidarity loses sight of subsidiarity, it "gives way to paternalist social assistance that is demeaning to those in need."[61] Organizations that build solidarity without subsidiarity risk creating cultures marked by conformity and excessive centralization. This may be expressed through a fixation on the investor or customer. The customer, for example, can become king, and employees and leaders indentured servants, exhausted and suffocating in a trap of their own making. Subsidiarity balanced with solidarity prevents a gradual devolution into uniformity and conformity.

60. When subsidiarity and solidarity work together, they complement and mutually enrich each other.[62] Solidarity signals *the social dimension of the person*, while subsidiarity signals *the personal dimension of societies*. Solidarity calls us to embrace the common good and human dignity collectively, as the good of all; while subsidiarity calls us to embrace the common good and human dignity "distributively," as the good of each. Mutually informed, each by the other, subsidiarity and solidarity create a synergy capable of supporting authentic, integral human development. Mind, body, and spirit are continually strengthened through social interaction and meaningful work. In this way, the whole person, the organization, and the larger society are all nourished.

The Interaction of Solidarity and Subsidiarity at Work

		LOW	HIGH
SOLIDARITY	HIGH	Paternal/Centralization	Integral Human Development
	LOW	Disengagement/Disassociation	Privatism/Localism
		SUBSIDIARITY	

CHAPTER 3

ACTING

Creating a Culture of Subsidiarity

61. INFORMED BY THE ELEMENTS of "Seeing" and "Judging," we can now describe the cultural agenda for leaders guided by subsidiarity under three headings: 1) *orienting* an organization's culture toward subsidiarity; 2) *institutionalizing* subsidiarity in the practices, policies, and structures of a company; 3) and *sustaining* subsidiarity for the organization's future.[63] It bears mentioning that aspects of this principle, taken one at a time, are familiar terms in the literature on management and organizational life. That there should be an alignment among management, social science, and theological thinkers may well point to the truth and substantial nature of the shared practices, attitudes, and concepts that we associate with subsidiarity. In any case, we repeat the confession of Sir Isaac Newton in this regard: "If I have seen a little further it is by standing on the shoulders of the Giants."[64]

Orienting: Three Leadership Responsibilities

62. **Person-Centered Work Design.** Leaders who wish to orient their organizations toward the principle of subsidiarity face three important orienting tasks. The first is to design work for employees in a way that taps their gifts, talents, and skills. Howard Rosenbrock, a manufacturing engineer, pointed out that too often engineers design work for people that requires only a fraction of their talents, skills, and knowledge. If they were to "consider people as though they were robots," he argued, they would try "to provide them with less trivial and more human work."[65] Most engineers, he explained, would reorganize the production process to make full use of a robot's potential. To do otherwise would not only be considered wasteful and inefficient, it would offend their sense of design!

63.   While work design must be person-centered, it also has to be organizationally effective. In the *Vocation of the Business Leader*, executives are advised to "design work that is good and effective, efficient and engaging, autonomous and collaborative." This allows companies to compete in the marketplace and helps people to flourish in their work.[66] Leaders of organizations need to define the boundaries of autonomy for the various parts of the business. This is a key leadership responsibility since it creates the right conditions for employees to understand their tasks, their degrees of freedom, and their interdependencies within the organization as a whole. Business units and departments need to know what their roles are, what types of results they are expected to achieve, and how they fit within the general strategy.

64.   One of the constant challenges facing businesses, especially larger ones, is that sub-units, departments, and divisions come to see themselves as autonomous, losing sight of the whole. This can be particularly problematic when external pressures force company-wide adaptation. A CEO of a $2 billion multinational corporation, who is explicitly attempting to operationalize subsidiarity, told us that when the 2008/2009 financial crisis hit, he had to move the business in a more top-down mode without destroying the shared trust and respect that he and his leaders had built with their employees. It was actually the shared trust, he said, that allowed leadership to take swift action to avoid financial ruin.[67]

65. **Employee Development.** The second orienting task for leaders is to develop the people that they lead. While it is true that when people bring their skills and knowledge into an organization they add to its "collective intelligence," this collective intelligence does not just happen of its own accord. To make subsidiarity work, Charles Handy argues, "The holders of the responsibilities, the repositories of subsidiarity if you like, have to be educated up to their responsibilities. You can't, responsibly, give responsibility to incompetents. On the other hand, those people will remain incompetent unless they have the incentive of responsibility. It has to be a chicken and egg process, in steps and by degrees."[68]

66. Subsidiarity presupposes "that people are an organization's most valuable resource and that a manager's job is to prepare and free people to perform."[69] An essential added benefit of this preparation is that it encourages employee engagement. Preparing people so they can perform helps them engage by fostering pride in their work. Embodied in an organizational culture, this view of people encourages employees to rise above self-interest and to work for the greater good, says executive Alison Chung. She views "*an ideal organization*" as "*one that brings out the best qualities in all of the individuals within the organization and has a synergistic effect to make it something a lot bigger than the individual parts.*"[70]

67. Leaders "assist" (*subsidium*) their people through effective education, training, mentoring, and counsel. In the context of the logic of gift, this is the special contribution of good leaders. They create an organization that fosters the effective development of employees equipping them with the tools, expertise, and experience needed to carry out their tasks. Defining employees' work broadly while neglecting to aid them in this manner is a recipe for failure—both for the employee and for the organization.

68. At Reell Precision Manufacturing, the company redesigned its assembly line from a Command-Direct-Control style of management in which management made all the decisions concerning the assembly area, to a Teach-Equip-Trust style of management in which employees were taught inspection procedures, equipped with quality instruments, and trusted to do things right on their own assembly line. By restructuring the work process according to the principle of subsidiarity, employees decreased set-up times for new products, reduced the need for quality inspection, increased overall quality, and required less supervision. By reducing these costs, the company not only created more humane work, but also created the conditions to increase their labor rates.

69. **Limited Delegation to Full Trust.** The third task for orienting a culture toward subsidiarity is to *establish strong relationships with employees*, beginning with delegation and moving to trust. We think of delegation in this context not simply in terms of its instrumental value for getting more work done, but as passing on authority incrementally toward full trust and confidence. This increases the capacities of individuals and the business as a whole. When business leaders accept responsibility for developing employees, delegation becomes more than a tool for efficiency. It becomes a mini-classroom for both leaders and employees. They test performance with increasing levels of risk and trust: from carrying out orders to independent choices where the costs of failure are low, to consultation and feedback (early stages), to full participation with leaders in decision making (advanced stages), and finally to independent problem solving (full trust).

70. Limited delegation may be interpreted to mean that the leader who gives the subordinate power might take it back at any time, reserving the right to accept or reject what the subordinate accomplishes.[71] Under limited delegation, employees, no matter how well they may perform, assume neither full risk nor full accountability for their actions because the leader has the final word. With full trust (and independent problem solving), employees are more likely to innovate and try new methods because they have the authority to do so; and they are likely to strive for excellence because they are accountable for their decisions.

71. Delegation, when used effectively, recognizes individual differences in readiness and in ability. It requires transparent and trusting relationships between leaders and those to whom they delegate. When employees exercise delegated authority competently, freely, and responsibly, bonds of trust between employees and leaders are reinforced. Even limited delegation can have benefits in any organization: by increasing employees' pride and ownership in their work, expanding their self-awareness and knowledge, and allowing them to demonstrate skills that signal leadership potential.[72]

72. Delegation is an indispensable tool for achieving an organization's desired economic and cultural goals—but it is only a tool. Subsidiarity, on the other hand, goes beyond instrumentality. It is a moral principle that points to two truths: namely that all people have gifts to be exercised and work to do, and that all authority should not and cannot reside with the leader. In a culture of subsidiarity, the focus is on the exercise of gifts and the growth of employees through their acceptance of responsibility. The leader committed to subsidiarity does not claim to own all the work and then allocate it through delegation so as to be more efficient. Rather, the leader recognizes that certain work belongs to employees and is theirs to manage. Charles Handy explains that subsidiarity "implies that the power properly belongs, in the first place, lower down or further out. You take it away as a last resort. Those in the center are the servants of the parts. The task of the center, and of any leader, is to help the individual or the group to live up to their responsibilities, to enable them to deserve their subsidiarity."[73] This requires the virtue of trust, a willingness to risk failure, and the patience to teach. Doing this well makes it more likely that the leader will be able to identify the right people for the right positions at the right time.

73. As a moral principle, subsidiarity reminds us that people develop as they exercise initiative, skill, and intelligence. The task of any leader is to help people do their work responsibly for the sake of the whole business. Leaders who truly embrace the principle of subsidiarity think of employees as coworkers and colleagues rather than simply as subordinates. They assume, as a virtuous habit, the risk of trusting employee decisions where experience has told them such trust is warranted. In doing so they neither abdicate prudential judgment nor trade it for naive acceptance of employee capabilities. Effective leaders avoid second-guessing employees and standing in critical judgment over them. They do not absolve themselves of accountability by blaming others for failures. Subsidiarity brooks no evasion or shirking: leaders and employees are always and every day in this together—failures, successes, and all.

Institutionalizing: Methods for Measuring and Strengthening Subsidiarity

74. A key to embedding the principle of subsidiarity in an organization's culture is to reinforce it in virtually every area of organizational life—in hiring practices; in employee evaluation, training, and promotion; in leadership-building exercises and formal communications of all types. As with any approach to continuous improvement, efforts to institutionalize subsidiarity require evidence-based assessment and serious, ongoing reflection. The following practices can help strengthen subsidiarity.

▶ **Training and Development Budgets and Policies.** The resources devoted to employee training and development are an indicator of the value that an organization attaches to subsidiarity. The useful information here is not so much the amount spent in a given year, but trends, ratio analyses, and proportionate resource allocation among key groups.

▶ **Formal Structures to Mediate Participation.** One critical gauge of subsidiarity is the degree to which an organization facilitates employee participation in decisions. In workplaces where subsidiarity is valued, employees exercise initiative through participation at all levels. Leaders of organizations that give real attention to new suggestions about work design help foster cultures that value the gifts of employees at every level. Business structures can be designed to enlist participation in many ways— with adjustments suited to the organization's industry and approach to production. Processes that encourage participation include: team-based work systems; shared management groups that provide employees the opportunity to shape the work flows in which they participate; and beginning-and-end-of-shift huddles, which permit employees to communicate with their peers about the current state of operations, immediate challenges to be addressed, and other vital issues.[74]

▶ **Percentages of Internal Promotions.** An organization's ability to find within its existing workforce the leadership skills that it seeks may indicate how deeply subsidiarity is institutionalized.

The extent to which it prepares employees for advancement to senior roles, and the percentage of such internal promotions are key indicators.

► **Rates of Employee Turnover in Relation to Self-Development.** In any organization, there is good turnover and bad turnover. Exit interviews may provide useful information about the reasons for employee departures. Reasons such as frustration with decision-making or lack of talent development opportunities, for example, may signal inadequate concern for subsidiarity.

► **Employee Engagement Surveys.** Annual surveys measuring employee satisfaction might also assess subsidiarity by looking at personal growth and engagement in the workplace. Such surveys could ask whether employees perceive they are respected by superiors and/or believe their concerns are taken seriously—for example, in the shaping of workflows. Similarly, these surveys could ask employees whether they have access to the tools and training they need to exercise decision-making responsibly.

► **Regular Communications about Subsidiarity.** Subsidiarity can be further institutionalized by highlighting its importance in organizational communications (newsletters, websites, and other media), providing examples of its historical presence in the organization, and offering illustrations of its current practice.

► **Empowerment and Interactive Leadership.** At a minimum, two key management skills are necessary for the practice of subsidiarity to succeed: empowerment and interactive leadership. Both skills have been identified as "distinctive and characteristic features of women in leadership positions," according to Judy Rosener, a fact that suggests an advantage for leadership teams that include both women and men. In addition to sharing power and authority, the idea of empowerment points to self-actualization as well. Interactive leadership finds its roots in participative management, and stresses, "1) encouragement of participation in all aspects of work; 2) wide-spread sharing of information and power; 3) efforts to enhance self-worth of employees; and 4) energizing employees for the task."[75]

▶ **Performance Evaluation.** While the old adage "What does not get measured does not get managed" has its limitations, it nonetheless highlights an important aspect of business leadership. No single metric or policy reveals whether subsidiarity is being lived out in an organization. Two areas of evaluation, however, signal the salience of subsidiarity: *individual* performance assessments and *institution-wide* assessments. At the *individual level*, managers should invite 360-degree feedback from subordinates as part of their performance reviews. This feedback should also include employee assessments of managers' respect for subordinates' gifts and talents. At the *institution-wide level*, techniques have been developed for periodic organizational self-assessment that allow evidence-based measurement of hard-to-measure cultural attributes.[76]

Sustaining: Providing Continuity for a Culture of Subsidiarity

75. The third stage of the cultural agenda for subsidiarity is about maintaining the commitment to this principle over time. An organization can fail at sustaining its commitment to subsidiarity in two ways: (1) *internally*, by hiring and promoting to leadership levels people who do not value subsidiarity—leading to the eventual erosion of this core value; or (2) succumbing to *external pressures* (such as competitive forces, market forces, government mandates, social pressures) that force a choice between survival and subsidiarity. Sustaining subsidiarity requires the implementation of practices that anticipate the problems of value erosion and external pressure and address them systematically before they become real threats. Attention to recruiting and hiring, succession planning, corporate governance, and strategic positioning are key in this endeavor.

▶ **Recruiting for Subsidiarity.** Recruiting and hiring both leaders and subordinates requires attention to more than basic job competencies. Eagerness and understanding when it comes to taking responsibility are equally important. A successful search process might include patiently passing over candidates showing weak signs of alignment with a culture of subsidiarity. These same considerations apply to promotion criteria. When leaders recruit people based both on competence *and* principle, they will receive a kind of "moral salary" that complements their economic salary. Moreover, subsidiarity can be a significant attractor and retainer in the realm of talent management. One way to discern subsidiarity in management candidates is to ask in their interviews about past decisions they have made: "Was it really up to you to take this or that decision? Why did you feel it necessary to take on this decision?" Similar questions can be asked about their views of the information required to manage: "Why do you need that information? Is it really absolutely necessary to exercise your own responsibilities or is it to control subordinates? In the latter case, why do you need to control? Is it a matter of trust? How confident are you that you have chosen the right person, trained that person effectively, and provided the employee with the right tools?"[77] Such questions can elicit a candidate's commitment to subsidiarity.

▶ **Succession Planning and Subsidiarity.** Senior leaders, especially those being groomed for promotion, routinely should be familiarized with the principle of subsidiarity, the organization's strategic and moral commitment to it, and the behaviors, attitudes, and decisions expected to support the pursuit of this communal good. If subsidiarity is alive and well in an organization, leadership succession from within typically will become easier, since the gifts of subordinates will be valued, engaged, and developed as a matter of course.

▶ **Boards of Directors: Membership and Functioning.** Directors need to take responsibility for the culture of the company over time. The board as a whole is responsible for the moral constraints attached to longer-term economic decisions. Its members play a critical role in identifying and recruiting new senior leaders and, when necessary, removing existing leaders. As organizational trustees, the board has a duty to reflect on how the company exhibits core values (such as subsidiarity and solidarity). Boards also benefit from vigilance in avoiding two temptations antithetical to subsidiarity: serving as a "rubberstamp" for senior executives and micromanaging.

▶ **Subsidiarity and the Surrounding Social Environment.** Threats from outside the company, either from the marketplace or from the public sector (government) call for different strategies. In the long term, subsidiarity supports both effective and efficient performance in the marketplace. But in crisis situations, decision makers are often pressured to assume a "command and control" mentality that can undermine subsidiarity. One of the most important challenges for leaders is to respond to pressure from clients or competitors without giving excessive ground on subsidiarity. Similar pressures arise from the public sector, when, for example, government agencies pressure companies to meet unreasonable deadlines or expectations for adhering to standards, regulations, or new laws.

76. In sum, an organization that *espouses* subsidiarity with conviction (orientation) and whose practices and processes *reinforce* it (institutionalization), can nevertheless fail to *sustain* a culture of subsidiarity if it fails to seriously attend to this core value when hiring and promoting employees, choosing board members, providing for leadership succession, and responding to external pressures.

CONCLUSION

77. Operationalizing subsidiarity is an important part of the vocation of the business leader. Like a compass, this principle points the way toward the creation of an organizational culture that fosters *good work* both in terms of the development of the employee and the productive capacity of the organization.[78] In today's business environment, however, practicing subsidiarity is not easy. Subsidiarity cannot be achieved only by a mechanical algorithm of managerial acts or attitudes, however practical or concrete. One size does not fit all. Neither is it an off-the-shelf approach to organizational problems; by definition, successful implementation requires the unique and relevant participation wherever it is tried.

78. Throughout this essay, we have pointed to the challenges leaders face in managing the sometimes contradictory pressures of organizational values associated with the principle of subsidiarity. Success in implementing subsidiarity requires a continuous, artful balancing of tensions created by the push and pull of these values. It also calls for practically wise, skilled leaders, who, focused on a vision of human flourishing, proceed toward this goal with creativity, patience, and perseverance. A critical task is to hold simultaneously, in a kind of golden tension, three sets of values inherent to subsidiarity:

▶ **Trust and Accountability.** Giving as much individual responsibility as possible and as much administrative support as necessary. As Charles Handy has noted, "trust has to be earned, but in order to be earned it has first to be given."[79] Trust does not mean "doing whatever you want," but neither does it mean "set aside your judgment and do only as directed." The way accountability is accomplished, in other words, can either undermine or increase trust.

- ▶ **Centralization and Decentralization.** Moving decision-making to *the lowest level possible and to the highest level necessary.* Any decisions or tasks that can realistically and reasonably be handled at the individual, departmental, or regional level should be authorized at that level; those that cannot should be handled at a higher level.

- ▶ **Standardization and Innovation.** Insisting upon as many standards as necessary but ensuring as much initiative and innovation as possible. While standards bring unity to organizational life, uniformity may stifle discovery and innovation.

79. These tensions inevitably grow and subside as organizational and competitive conditions change. But when embraced prudently, they have the potential to create a dynamic culture enlivened by subsidiarity and the fruits of its practice, among them good work. Effective business managers understand the meaning of good work.[80] This is not an undertaking apart from, or in addition to, the roles of management; it is, in our view, a vital and integral part of what defines good work both for the leader and the employee. Nor do we regard the practice of subsidiarity as benefitting only or even primarily the business itself. To the extent that the experience of work life contributes to the fulfillment of individual employees who also have families and contribute to their communities; to the extent that it helps them develop and exercise their minds and their talents, their confidence and their sense of personal accountability; to the extent that work and the culture of subsidiarity contributes to the development of persons, it also contributes to the common good.

80. In closing, we return to the theological beginnings of the principle of subsidiarity, rooted in the idea of the human person gifted by the Creator as an expression of *imago Dei*, and whose very work, therefore, is an act of co-creation. The leader informed by subsidiarity and demonstrating *respect in action* arouses in his or her employees a deep sense of their own gifted capacities for work, for accomplishment. Thus respected and affirmed employees may also be inspired to act with generous hearts in service to others.[81] For the leader who sees employees in this light, every effort to create an environment where human gifts can be more fully realized and where co-creation can be more concretely expressed is a noble effort. For such a leader, the principle of subsidiarity is more than a way to design good work, or to make good products, or to offer good services. It is a way to enlarge the possibilities for full human development at work, indeed, for people to become who they were created to be.

AFTERWORD

THE IDEA FOR THIS ESSAY originated with Pierre Lecocq (see his foreword). Pierre collaborated on the drafting committee of the Pontifical Council for Justice and Peace's document *Vocation of the Business Leader* (2012). In writing that document, his business experience and faith perspective brought into clearer light the importance of subsidiarity and its relationship to business. For the first time in a Vatican document, subsidiarity was associated with businesses and not just with the state. While the section was short (four paragraphs), it highlighted the need to examine this relationship between subsidiarity and business in greater depth.

In March 2013, Pierre and I along with other representatives of UNIAPAC met in Beirut, Lebanon, on the occasion of the UNIAPAC Beirut Conference, where the Arabic version of the *Vocation of the Business Leader* was launched. Here, Pierre identified and articulated the need to expand the section on subsidiarity and provide a more systematic expression of subsidiarity as a leadership principle for businesspeople. Since then, we have created a unique relationship between a "practitioner" institution (UNIAPAC) and an "academic" institution (University of St. Thomas, Minnesota) and together, we produced this document on subsidiarity.

Over the past two years, my colleagues from the University of St. Thomas, Ken Goodpaster, Jeanne Buckeye, and Dean Maines, and I have written this essay in dialogue with Pierre as well as dozens of other practitioners and academics. We have sought to learn from the practical experience of leaders and their organizations as well as draw upon the wisdom of a social tradition that is over two thousand years old. Combining the practice of lived experience and the wisdom of tradition imbues a "practical wisdom" on how to create "good work" in today's organizations.

We are clearly in need of this unique integration between lived, practical experience and a wisdom tradition that generates moral and spiritual principles. Too often theology and philosophy are seen as abstractions that are either so distant they do not land anywhere, or so privatized that they have no expression in the world of work. And too often businesses and their leaders are so focused on the practical that they instrumentalize everything, including relationships, so as to achieve purely financial results.

This relationship between the practical and principle has been expressed within Christianity and in particular in the Catholic social tradition's complementary relationship among authoritative teachers (Catholic social teachings), insightful scholars (Catholic social thought), and effective and principled practitioners (Catholic social practice). As a three-legged stool, it is a wisdom tradition constantly developing, purifying, and readjusting itself as it seeks to discern the good in social life; in essence it is a living wisdom. This essay is one contribution to the important reflection on this complementary relationship and seeks to express what highly principled business leaders look like in today's complex economy. We have done this by using a classic method within the Catholic social tradition of "see, judge, act," which was also used in the *Vocation of the Business Leader.*

Our hope for this essay is that it will inspire leaders to reflect on the principle of subsidiarity and its benefits and challenges in organizational practice. We also hope it will generate more reflection, case studies, and research on subsidiarity as a principle of leadership. As we move into an increasingly secular culture evermore dependent upon technology, we are prone to reduce our work to merely a series of techniques that measure greater increases in profitability and productivity. Without strong principles rooted in moral and spiritual soil, we lose sight of the human person and see business as simply a utilitarian exchange of economic costs and benefits. Subsidiarity calls us out of this financial fixation and raises our vision to see employees gifted by the Creator as an expression of the *imago Dei*, and whose very work, therefore, is an act of co-creation. For the leader who sees persons in this light, every effort to create an environment where human gifts can be more fully realized and where co-creation can be more beautifully expressed is a noble effort. For such a leader the principle of subsidiarity is more than a way to design good work, or make good products, or offer good services. It is a way to enlarge the possibilities for full human flourishing, indeed, for people to become who they were created to be through the work they do and the life-giving culture their work helps to build.

Michael J. Naughton
Interim Director of the Center for Catholic Studies,
    University of St. Thomas
Board Chair, Reell Precision Manufacturing
St. Paul, Minnesota, January 2015

CONTRIBUTOR NOTES

Jeanne G. Buckeye is associate professor at the University of St. Thomas in St. Paul, Minnesota in the Opus College of Business, Department of Ethics and Business Law, where she teaches both MBA and undergraduate students. Her regular courses include Business Ethics, Reflective Management, the Great Books, and Faith and the Management Profession. In addition to teaching, she serves as Interim Director of the John A. Ryan Institute for Catholic Social Thought at St. Thomas and co-coordinator of the Great Books Seminar. Buckeye is coauthor with John B. Gallagher of *Structures of Grace: Business Practices of the Economy of Communion*, published in 2014. In her years at UST she has also served in administrative positions, including associate dean and acting dean of graduate business programs. She earned an MBA and a PhD in Management from the University of Minnesota.

Kenneth E. Goodpaster earned his AB in mathematics from the University of Notre Dame and his AM and PhD in philosophy from the University of Michigan. Goodpaster taught graduate and undergraduate philosophy at the University of Notre Dame throughout the 1970s before joining the Harvard Business School faculty in 1980, where he developed the ethics curriculum. In 1990 Goodpaster left Harvard to accept the David and Barbara Koch Endowed Chair in Business Ethics at the University of St. Thomas. At St. Thomas, he has taught in the full-time and part-time MBA programs. His publications include *Conscience and Corporate Culture* (Wiley-Blackwell, 2007) and *Policies and Persons: A Casebook in Business Ethics* (McGraw-Hill, 2006). He also contributed to the *Vocation of the Business Leader*, issued by the Pontifical Council for Justice and Peace (2012). Most recently Goodpaster served as executive editor of a much-anticipated history, *Corporate Responsibility: The American Experience* (Cambridge University Press, 2012), which received the 2014 Academy of Management Best Book Award. He was recently named to *Ethisphere Magazine*'s annual list of the *100 Most Influential People in Business Ethics*. Goodpaster is now professor emeritus in the Opus College of Business.

T. Dean Maines is the president of the Veritas Institute at the University of St. Thomas. He also is co-coordinator of the Great Books Seminar offered by the Opus College of Business. Prior to assuming leadership of the Veritas Institute, Maines served as the research associate to the Koch Chair in Business Ethics. Before joining the University of St. Thomas, Maines spent sixteen years in various capacities for Cummins, Inc., including chief human resource executive for the firm's worldwide Power Generation Group and president of the Columbus Occupational Health Association, Inc. Maines was a Sloan Fellow at Stanford University's Graduate School of Business, where he earned a MS in management. He also holds an AB in philosophy and a BS in mechanical engineering from Cornell University. Articles on corporate ethics authored and coauthored by Maines have appeared in the *Business and Professional Ethics Journal, European Financial Review, Health Progress, HEC Forum,* the *Journal of Catholic Higher Education,* the *Journal of Corporate Citizenship,* the *Journal of Management Development, Risk Management,* and *Science and Engineering Ethics.* He also has contributed to *B. Magazine,* the *Journal of International Business, MX Magazine,* the *Palgrave Handbook of Spirituality and Business,* and the *Sage Encyclopedia of Business Ethics and Society*.

Michael J. Naughton is currently the interim director of the Center for Catholic Studies. He is the holder of the Alan W. Moss Endowed Chair in Catholic Social Thought at the University of St. Thomas where he is full professor with a joint appointment in the departments of Catholic Studies (College of Arts and Sciences) and Ethics and Business Law (Opus College of Business). He is the coauthor and coeditor of nine books and over forty articles. He helped coordinate and write the *Vocation of the Business Leader* issued by the Pontifical Council for Justice and Peace (2012), which has been translated into fifteen languages. Naughton serves as board chair for Reell Precision Manufacturing, a global producer of innovative torque solutions for transportation, consumer electronics, medical, and office automation products. He has also served on the board of several nonprofit organizations including Seeing Things Whole. He received his PhD in theology from Marquette University (1991) and an MBA from the University of St. Thomas (1995). He is married with five children.

INSTITUTIONAL SPONSORS

UNIAPAC IS A FEDERATION OF ASSOCIATIONS, an international meeting place for Christian business leaders. Its full name is the "International Christian Union of Business Executives." Originally created in 1931 in Europe, it is an international nonprofit association headquartered in Paris. It gathers thirty-seven associations from thirty-five countries in Europe, Latin America, Africa, and Asia, grouping fifteen thousand business leaders. It is an ecumenical organization. Inspired by Christian social thought, its goal is to promote among business leaders the vision and implementation of an economy serving the human person and the common good of humanity at large. UNIAPAC functions in terms of both its associations and its international office.

UNIAPAC Associations Mission

▶ To contribute to public debates on contemporary social issues triggered by new technological advances and economic growth in different regions of the world as a mean to focus attention on the crucial need to show the upmost respect to the human person in all circumstances.
▶ To support the personal transformation of its members and through them the transformation of their companies and their business environment.

UNIAPAC International Mission

▶ To represent these associations in the international institutions dealing with global economic and social issues.
▶ To serve as a link between Christian associations of business exec-

utives across the world, to promote and facilitate exchanges between them, and to furnish a common mouthpiece if and when the need arises.

▶ To support the activities of these national and regional associations.

▶ To sponsor the founding of Christian associations of business executives, where none exists.

▶ To seize any opportunity and to promote any venture that will contribute to the realization of these objectives.

Located in Paris (www.uniapac.org), UNIAPAC's governance is assured by an international board composed of the presidents of the member associations meeting twice a year, and an executive board composed of the UNIAPAC president, the presidents of the regional organizations (Europe, Latin America, and Africa), and a spiritual adviser.

University of St. Thomas

The University of St. Thomas is a Catholic, liberal arts, and professional institution of approximately ten thousand students in the US in the state of Minnesota. Grounded in the Catholic intellectual tradition, an important part of the work of the university is "educating highly principled global business leaders." This work is in part expressed through the Center for Catholic Studies' John A. Ryan Institute for Catholic Social Thought and the Opus College of Business' Veritas Institute. Below is a brief description of both institutes.

▶ **The John A. Ryan Institute for Catholic Social Thought** of the Center for Catholic Studies explores the relationship between the Catholic social tradition and business theory and practice by fostering a deeper integration of faith and work. The Ryan Institute has become an important voice in Catholic higher education by helping to build a community of scholars and practitioners dedicated to examining issues at the intersection of business and the Catholic social tradition. Four principal activities make up its work: research, faculty development, curricular development, and leadership outreach. In collaboration with other educational institutions worldwide, the Ryan Institute organizes conferences, seminars, faculty-development programs, and curricular and research projects. Themes of this work have focused on the purpose of business, the vocation and spirituality of the leader, wealth creation and distribution, poverty and prosperity, and mission-driven business education. With an international community of scholars and practitioners, it has organized twelve international conferences around the world including the Philippines, India, Italy, Vatican, Spain, Belgium, Germany, Mexico, and the US. It also has facilitated within St. Thomas approximately twenty seminars for new faculty, administrators, staff, and business faculty since 1997. The Institute has published books and articles in a variety of academic journals and presses and has over five hundred papers on the relationship of business and Catholic social thought on its website (www.stthomas.edu/cathstudies/cst/).

▶ **The Veritas Institute of the Opus College of Business** promotes ethically responsible organizational conduct through systematic assessment. Application of the Institute's assessment tools enables for-profit and not-for-profit firms to integrate ethical principles more effectively within their management systems. This helps organizations to better align their decisions and actions with their professed moral beliefs. The reflection and learning that results from use of the Institute's tools also aids the development of effective, ethical leaders, and helps firms to advance the common good through a positive impact upon the broader society. One of the Institute's tools, the *Catholic Identity Matrix*, is a recognized best practice within Catholic healthcare. The *Catholic Identity Matrix* has been utilized by over sixty Catholic hospitals in the United States, Germany, and Mexico. The Institute also promotes research concerning the institutionalization of moral values within organizations. In addition, it organizes events and conferences that explore topics in corporate ethics that touch upon multiple dimensions—the individual, the enterprise, and society. The Institute is administrative home of the *Great Books Seminar*, a unique graduate elective offered by the Opus College of Business that is based upon the world-renowned Aspen Institute Executive Seminar. More information about the Institute may be found on its website (http://www.stthomas.edu/centers/veritas/).

ENDNOTES

1. Twitter post, June 24, 2014, 2:24 a.m., accessed December 16, 2014, https://twitter.com/Pontifex/status/481367133494865922.

2. William Pollard, *The Soul of the Firm* (Downers Grove, IL: HarperBusiness, 1996), 102.

3. The document *Vocation of the Business Leader* speaks of three interdependent goods of business: good goods, good work, and good wealth. Sections on good work (44–50) highlight the principle of subsidiarity. Pontifical Council for Justice and Peace, *Vocation of the Business Leader: A Reflection* (*VBL*), 3rd Edition (St. Paul, MN: John A. Ryan Institute for Catholic Social Thought, 2012), accessed December 16, 2014, http://www.stthomas.edu/VBL.

4. Benedict XVI, *Caritas in Veritate*, 2009, §57, accessed December 16, 2014, http://www.vatican.va/holy_father/benedict_xvi/encyclicals/documents/hf_ben-xvi_enc_20090629_caritas-in-veritate_en.html. John XXIII, in his encyclical *Mater et Magistra*, echoes this point as well: "Consequently, if the whole structure and organization of an economic system is such as to compromise human dignity, to lessen a man's sense of responsibility or rob him of opportunity for exercising personal initiative, then such a system, We maintain, is altogether unjust—no matter how much wealth it produces, or how justly and equitably such wealth is distributed" (1961, §83), accessed December 16, 2014, http://www.vatican.va/holy_father/john_xxiii/encyclicals/documents/hf_j-xxiii_enc_15051961_mater_en.html.

5. Peter F. Drucker, *The Effective Executive: The Definitive Guide to Getting the Right Things Done* (New York: HarperCollins, 2006), 168.

6. Charles A. O'Reilly and Jeffrey Pfeffer, *Hidden Value: How Great Companies Achieve Extraordinary Results with Ordinary People* (Boston: Harvard Business School Press, 2000), 82. Derek Salman Pugh and David

John Hickson, *Great Writers on Organizations: The Third Omnibus Edition* (Aldershot [etc.]: Ashgate, 2007).

7. Peter B. Vaill, *Managing as a Performing Art: New Ideas for a World of Chaotic Change* (San Francisco: Jossey-Bass, 1989).

8. Charles B. Handy, "Subsidiarity Is the Word for It," *Across the Board* 36, no. 6 (1999): 7–8. Pius XI, *Quadragesimo Anno*, 1931, §79, accessed December 16, 2014, http://www.vatican.va/holy_father/pius_xi /encyclicals/documents/hf_p-xi_enc_19310515_quadragesimo-anno _en.html.

9. Russell Hittinger, "Social Pluralism and Subsidiarity in Catholic Social Doctrine," *Annales Theologici* 16 (2002): 385–408. When referring to decision making, Hittinger emphasizes, "*First*, the principle [of subsidiarity] does not require [placing decision making at the] 'lowest possible level' but rather the 'proper level'" (396).

10. We are particularly grateful to Kyle Smith for this insight.

11. See John XXIII, *Mater et Magistra*, §236. See Josef Pieper, *The Four Cardinal Virtues* (Notre Dame: University of Notre Dame Press, 1966), 10. See also Timothy M. Gallagher, OMV, *The Discernment of Spirits: An Ignatian Guide for Everyday Living* (Chestnut Ridge: Crossroad Publishing, 2005), 16–26.

12. Mary Midgley, "On Trying Out One's New Sword," in *Heart and Mind: The Varieties of Moral Experience* (New York: St. Martin's Press, 1981), 72.

13. Ibid.

14. John Paul II, *Centesimus Annus*, 1991, §11 and §46, accessed January 21, 2015, http://www.vatican.va/holy_father/john_paul_ii/encyclicals /documents/hf_jp-ii_enc_01051991_centesimus-annus_en.html.

15. Gallup, Inc., "The 12 Elements of Great Managing," in *Employee Engagement: What's Your Engagement Ratio?* (2010): 2, accessed December 16, 2014, http://www.americasdiversityleader.com/Downloads/Employee_Engagement_Overview_Brochure.pdf. Barb Sanford, "'The High Cost of Disengaged Employees,' A Q&A with Curt Coffman, Global Practice Leader for Q12 Management Consulting," *Gallup Business Jour-*

nal (April 15, 2002), accessed December 16, 2014, http://businessjournal.gallup.com/content/247/high-cost-disengaged-employees.aspx. Gallup, Inc., *State of the American Workplace: Employee Engagement Insights for U.S. Business Leaders* (Washington, DC, 2013), accessed July 18, 2013, http://www.gallup.com/strategicconsulting/163007/state-american-workplace.aspx.

16.   Gallup, Inc., *State of the American Workplace*, 5, 8–9, 12, accessed July 18, 2013, http://www.gallup.com/strategicconsulting/163007/state -american-workplace.aspx.

17.   See ILO's Decent Work Agenda, International Labour Organization (2013), accessed December 15, 2014, http://www.ilo.org/global /topics/decent-work/lang--en/index.htm and http://www.ilo.org /global/about-the-ilo/lang--en/index.htm.

18.   Kurt Hoover and Wallace T. Fowler, Report: "Studies in Ethics, Safety, and Liability for Engineers." One of six studies in the Report: "Doomed from the Beginning: The Solid Rocket Boosters for the Space Shuttle." Texas Space Grant Consortium Website at The University of Texas at Austin (1991), accessed November 19, 2014, http://www.tsgc.utexas. edu/archive/general/ethics/boosters.html. In his July 31, 1985, Inter-office Memo to R. K. Lund, Vice President of Engineering at Morton Thiokol, Inc., Roger Boisjoly (an engineer) wrote, "In my opinion, the team must be officially given the responsibility and the authority to execute the work that needs to be done on a non-interference basis (full time assignment until completed.) [*sic*] It is my honest and very real fear that if we do not take immediate action to dedicate a team to solve the problem with the field joint having the number one priority, then we stand in jeopardy of losing a flight along with all the launch pad facilities." Earlier in his memo, Boisjoly referred to a scenario with the O-rings, stating, "The result would be a catastrophe of the highest order—loss of human life." Roger Boisjoly, "Memo on O-Ring Erosion," posted on the Online Ethics Center for Engineering Website, August 29, 2006, National Academy of Engineering. Accessed December 16, 2014, http://www.onlineethics.org/cms/12703.aspx.

19. Gary Hamel and Bill Breen, *The Future of Management* (Boston: Harvard Business School Press, 2007), 91.

20. For a summary of Deming's 14 Points on Total Quality Management see http://asq.org/learn-about-quality/total-quality-management/overview/deming-points.html, accessed December 16, 2016.

21. See Christopher Bartlett and Sumantra Ghoshal's article, "Changing the Role of Top Management: Beyond Strategy to Purpose," *Harvard Business Review* 72, no. 6 (November–December 1994): 79–88.

22. The authors are indebted to André Delbecq's insights from "Subsidiarity and Contemporary Organization Theory" delivered at the 1st Mazatlán Forum, March 8, 2013, Mazatlán, Mexico, unpublished.

23. Bartlett and Ghoshal, "Changing the Role of Top Management: Beyond Strategy to Purpose," 81.

24. The ideal for "collective intelligence" came from a conversation we had with Vincent Lenhardt.

25. Domènec Melé, "The Principle of Subsidiarity in Organizations: A Case Study." Working Paper. IESE, DI-566-E (September, 2004), accessed December 16, 2014, http://www.iese.edu/research/pdfs/DI-0566-E.pdf. "Exploring the Principle of Subsidiarity in Organisational Forms," *Journal of Business Ethics* 60, no. 3 (2005): 293–305. For more on Melé's work with Fremap, see Pati Provinske's Annotated Bibliography.

26. John Paul II, *Centesimus Annus*, 1991, §11 and §46, accessed January 21, 2015, http://www.vatican.va/holy_father/john_paul_ii/encyclicals/documents/hf_jp-ii_enc_01051991_centesimus-annus_en.html.

27. Pierpaolo Donati discusses semantics to provide an understanding of the principle (211) in "What Does 'Subsidiarity' Mean? The Relational Perspective," *Journal of Markets & Morality* 12, no. 2 (2009): 211–43.

28. Benedict XVI, *Caritas in Veritate*, §57. John Finnis comments on subsidiarity:

    > It affirms that the proper function of association is to help the participants in the association to help themselves or, more precisely, to constitute themselves through the individual initiatives of choos-

ing commitments . . . and of realizing these commitments through personal inventiveness and effort in projects (many of which will, of course, be co-operative in execution and even communal in purpose). And since in large organizations the process of decision-making is more remote from the initiative of most of those many members who will carry out the decision, the same principle requires that larger associations should not assume functions which can be performed efficiently by smaller associations. . . . Human good requires not only that one *receive* and *experience* benefits or desirable states; it requires that one *do* certain things, that one should *act*, with integrity and authenticity; [. . .] Only in action . . . does one fully participate in human goods (John M. Finnis, *Natural Law and Natural Rights* [Oxford: Clarendon Press, 1980], 146–47).

29. Pius XI, *Quadragesimo Anno*, §79 and §80.

30. John J. Kelley, *Freedom in the Church: A Documented History of the Principle of Subsidiary Function* (Dayton, OH: Peter Li, 2000), 14.

31. Adam Smith, *The Wealth of Nations* (Chicago: University of Chicago Press, 1976), 302–03.

32. Alexis de Tocqueville, *Democracy in America* (New York: Anchor Press, 1969), 555–56.

33. Frederick Winslow Taylor, *The Principles of Scientific Management* (New York: Harper and Brothers, 1911).

34. Taylor, *The Principles of Scientific Management*, 36.

35. *Modern Times* was a 1936 comedy film written and directed by Charlie Chaplin in which his iconic "Little Tramp" character struggled to survive in the modern, industrialized world. The film is a comment on the desperate employment and fiscal conditions many people faced during the Great Depression, conditions created, in Chaplin's view, by the efficiencies of modern industrialization. See *Modern Times*, Charlie Chaplin (CA: United Artists, 1936).

36. Pius XI, *Quadragesimo Anno*, §135, emphasis added. While Catholic social thought has highlighted the importance of good work, there were occasional disputes between its members over its importance.

For example, Dorothy Day criticized Cardinal Cardijn for not taking seriously the importance of job design. Mark and Louise Zwick explain that

> while she agreed with his concern for factory workers, Dorothy disagreed with the idea of sanctifying one's work on an assembly line, insisting that the work itself must be changed so that the workers could be treated as human beings. She could not accept that workers who were laboring under inhuman conditions should simply be told that the way to holiness was to pray while they were working. She cried out: "What is the great disaster is that priests and laity alike have lost the concept of work, they have lost a philosophy of labor. . . . Those who do not know what work in a factory is, have romanticized both it and the workers, and in emphasizing the dignity of the worker, have perhaps unconsciously emphasized the dignity of work which is slavery, and which degrades and dehumanizes man. . . . Can one sanctify a saloon, a house of ill fame? When one is in the occasion of sin, is it not necessary to remove oneself from it? . . . In the great clean shining factories, with good lights and air and the most sanitary conditions, an eight-hour day, five-day week, with the worker chained to the belt, to the machine, there is no opportunity for sinning as the outsider thinks of sin. No, it is far more subtle than that, it is submitting oneself to a process which degrades, dehumanizes (Mark Zwick and Louise Zwick, *The Catholic Worker Movement: Intellectual and Spiritual Origins* [New York: Paulist Press, 2005], 164).

37. Giovanni Montini, "Letter to the 25th Italian Social Week," *l.c.*, col. 1356–1357, quoted in Calvez and Perrin (246). Montini would soon become Pope Paul VI. Jean-Yves Calvez and Jacques Perrin, *The Church and Social Justice: The Social Teaching of the Popes from Leo XIII to Pius XII (1878–1958)* (Chicago: Henry Regnery Company, 1961).

38. One reviewer of an earlier draft of this essay shared the following excerpts from John Ruskin in his book, *The Stones of Venice*, about the effects of menial labor and factory work:

[men] feel that the kind of labour to which they are condemned is verily a degrading one, and makes them less than men. [. . .] This, nature bade not,—this, God blesses not,—this, humanity for no long time is able to endure. We have much studied and much perfected, of late, the great civilized invention of the division of labour; only we give it a false name. It is not, truly speaking, the labour that is divided; but the men: —Divided into mere segments of men— broken into small fragments and crumbs of life; so that all the little piece of intelligence that is left in a man is not enough to make a pin, or a nail, but exhausts itself in making the point of a pin or the head of a nail (John Ruskin, "The Nature of the Gothic," in *On Art and Life* [New York: Penguin Books, 2005], 17–18. Ruskin's "Nature" was first published in *The Stones of Venice*, Vol. 2, 1853).

39. John Paul II, *Laborem Exercens*, 1981, §4. This is a paraphrasing of *VBL* rather than a verbatim quotation, see http://www.vatican.va/holy _father/john_paul_ii/encyclicals/documents/hf_jp-ii_enc_14091981 _laborem-exercens_en.html, accessed December 16, 2014.

40. See Benedict XVI, where he states: "Economic science tells us that structural insecurity generates anti-productive attitudes wasteful of human resources, inasmuch as workers tend to adapt passively to automatic mechanisms, rather than to release creativity. . . . *Human costs always include economic costs*, and economic dysfunctions always involve human costs" (§32), accessed December 16, 2014, http://www.vatican. va/holy_father/benedict_xvi/encyclicals/documents/hf_ben-xvi _enc_20090629_caritas-in-veritate_en.html. See also Wolfgang Grassl and André Habisch, "Ethics and Economics: Towards a New Humanistic Synthesis for Business," *Journal of Business Ethics* 99, no. 1 (February 2011): 37–49. Special issue on the 16th Annual International Conference Promoting Business Ethics.

41. Kenneth E. Goodpaster reflects on *Caritas in Veritate* (10) in "Goods That Are Truly Good and Services That Truly Serve: Reflections on '*Caritas in Veritate*,'" *Journal of Business Ethics* 100, no. S1 (2011): 9–16.

42. Lynn Sharp Paine, "Does Ethics Pay?" *Business Ethics Quarterly* 10, no. 1 (2000): 327. Paine adds in her conclusion: "Today's confidence that 'ethics pays' is a welcome advance from 'ethics is a luxury we can't afford.' Appreciation of the interdependencies between ethics and economic outcomes can only help to strengthen both. Nevertheless, 'ethics pays' is in its own way troubling as a credo for business leaders in the 21st century" (329).

43. T. S. Eliot, *Murder in the Cathedral* (New York: Harcourt, Brace & World, 1935), 44.

44. Russell Hittinger explains the similarities and differences found with Catholic and liberal understandings of subsidiarity:

> While liberals valued civil society principally for instrumental (the power-checking-power) reasons, Catholic social thought emphasized the intrinsic value of social forms like the family, the private school, churches, and labor unions. In the second place, Catholic social thought has always been suspicious of the market model of social pluralism. Though Catholic thinkers would have no difficulty defending the economic market against Socialism, they remained wary of any effort to make society itself conform to a market. [...] In order to appreciate how the ideas of social pluralism and subsidiarity can harbor quite different social ontologies, we shall investigate the idea of the *munus regale*—the function, mission, gift, or vocation of ruling. As we shall see, the *munus regale* originated in theological reflection upon the sacred offices of Christ as priest, prophet, and king, and how these *munera* are participated by every baptised person. Since the pontificate of Pius XI (1922–1939), the theme of the *munus regale* was applied beyond its original christological and ecclesiological boundaries to the offices, rights, and duties of social institutions. Especially in the social doctrine expounded by this papal magisterium, the idea of the *munus regale* is a keystone for understanding why the liberal conception of civil liberties, rights, and social pluralism needs to be preserved and corrected by an ontology of the human person as a "royal creature" who participates in divine ruling powers ("Pluralism and Subsidiarity," 388–89).

45. See Jacques Maritain, *Man and the State* (Chicago: University of Chicago Press, 1951), 77.

46. Russell Hittinger explains that the key to the development of the use of the principle of subsidiarity in Catholic social teaching hinges on the meaning of *munera*, which is often translated as one's function, but would be better translated as gifts, vocation, or mission. He writes:

> Pius XI decided to make clear that rights are not derived from human nature abstractly considered, but rather from human nature as already bearing (implicitly or explicitly) social *munera*. On this view, rights flow from antecedent *munera* (gifts, duties, vocations, missions); hence, it is quite different than the idea of a right as an immunity—*immunitas*, etymologically, implies the absence of a *munus*. It is quite true that immunities are a juridical term of art; every well-developed legal system recognizes immunities of various sorts. Pius XI, however, insisted that principles of social order cannot begin with immunities or with negative rights. We first must understand the *munera* which the immunities protect ("Pluralism and Subsidiarity," 393).

47. Hittinger explains that

> Pius XI . . . to whom we attribute the teachings on social justice and subsidiarity, is the pope who began to systematically develop the ontology of the *munera* [gift, vocation, mission, function]. During his pontificate, individuals, families, corporations, churches, the state itself, and even international authorities, were said to be the bearers not only of *iura* (rights) but also of *munera*—of having roles to play, gifts to give. In the deepest sense, human rights are exemplified in *munera*, whether natural or supernatural. In the Pian encyclicals, the concept of subsidiarity is elucidated first in the idea of a plurality of *munera*, and only secondarily in terms related to the political question of the scope and content of state assistance. Thus, the notion of the *munus* unifies two things which are so often split apart in modern political and social thought: first, what man claims as his own, and second, what man has to give as a gift of service ("Pluralism and Subsidiarity," 390–91).

As noted in Pati Provinske's Annotated Bibliography, Hittinger refers to Pius XI in *Divini Redemptoris* (1937), §31; Pius XII in *Summi Pontificatus* (1939); John XXIII in *Pacem in Terris* (1963), §68, §77, §141, and §145.

48. *Gaudium et Spes*, 1965, §24, accessed December 16, 2014, http://www .vatican.va/archive/hist_councils/ii_vatican_council/documents /vat-ii_cons_19651207_gaudium-et-spes_en.html.

49. For one expression of this logic, see Reell Precision Manufacturing's Direction Statement: "Instead of driving each other toward excellence, we strive to free each other to grow and express the excellence that is within all of us. [. . .] In our understanding of excellence we embrace a commitment to continuous improvement in everything we do. It is our commitment to encourage, teach, equip, and free each other to do and become all that we were intended to be," accessed January 5, 2015, http://reell.com/about/philosophy.

50. It is important to emphasize that human gifts cannot be detached from their use for the true good of both self and others. Clearly *conscience* comes into play when people's gifts are used, and when conscience is uncultivated and unformed, aberrations can and do occur. In the words of Joseph Ratzinger (before he became Pope Benedict XVI): "It is never wrong to follow the convictions one has arrived at—in fact, one *must* do so. But it can very well be wrong to have come to such askew convictions *in the first place*, by having stifled the protest of [conscience]. [. . .] For this reason, criminals of conviction like Hitler and Stalin are guilty" (38, emphasis added). Ratzinger's essay, "Conscience and Truth" can be found in *On Conscience*, ed. Edward J. Furton (Philadelphia, PA: The National Bioethics Center, 2007), 11–41. He presented his essay at the 10th Workshop for Bishops, February 1991, Dallas, Texas.

51. Vaclav Havel, "The Miracle of Being: Our Mysterious Interdependence," reprinted from *Sunrise Magazine*, October/November 1994, Theosophical University Press. See http://www.theosophy-nw.org /theosnw/issues/gl-hav1.htm, accessed December 16, 2014.

52. "Any breach in this dialogue [of faith and reason] comes only at an

enormous price to human development" (Benedict XVI, *Caritas in Veritate*, §56).

53. John Paul II, *Laborem Exercens*, §4 and §25.

54. *Catechism of the Catholic Church*, cross references 307 and 302 (Vatican: Libreria Editrice, 1884). The *Catechism* goes on to state that "This mode of governance ought to be followed in social life. The way God acts in governing the world, which bears witness to such great regard for human freedom, should inspire the wisdom of those who govern human communities. They should behave as ministers of divine providence," accessed December 16, 2014, http://www.vatican.va/archive/ccc_css/archive/catechism/p3s1c2a1.htm.

55. We are grateful to Fr. Michael Keating for this insight.

56. D. H. Lawrence, *Studies in Classic American Literature* (New York: Penguin Books, 1923), 12–13.

57. *VBL*, 2012, §4.

58. Benedict XVI, for example, explains that "the principle of subsidiarity must remain closely linked to the principle of solidarity and vice versa" (*Caritas in Veritate,* §58).

59. Ibid.

60. Rob Goffee and Gareth Jones, "Creating the Best Workplace on Earth," *Harvard Business Review* (May 2013): 108.

61. Benedict XVI, *Caritas in Veritate,* §58.

62. In addressing the meaning of subsidiarity, Donati writes, "We must examine how these principles can and should work together. As a matter of fact, solidarity and subsidiarity are mutually reinforcing and necessary to realizing the common good" (215). Pierpaolo Donati, "What Does 'Subsidiarity' Mean? The Relational Perspective," *Journal of Markets & Morality* 12, no. 2 (Fall 2009): 211–43. ISSN: 1098–1217.

63. See Kenneth E. Goodpaster, T. Dean Maines, and Arnold M. Weimerskirch (244), "A Baldrige Process for Ethics?" *Science and Engineering Ethics* 10, no. 2 (2004): 243–58. "Progressive articulation" is explained as providing successively more concrete and specific interpretations of high-level principles, enabling individuals and organizations

to apply them with more precision and less ambiguity (247–50). Goodpaster refers to orienting, institutionalizing, and sustaining (222–26) in "Ethical Imperatives and Corporate Leadership" in *Ethics in Practice*, ed. Kenneth R. Andrews (Boston: Harvard Business School Press), 212–28. Goodpaster's paper was first presented as the Ruffin Lecture in Business Ethics at the Darden Graduate School of Business Administration, University of Virginia, in April 1988.

64. Jean-Pierre Maury, *Newton: Understanding the Cosmos* (London: Thames and Hudson, 1992), 117.

65. Howard H. Rosenbrock, "Engineers and the Work That People Do," 5. This article was first published in IEEE *Control Systems Magazine* 1, no. 3, September. It was reprinted in *The Experience of Work*, ed. Craig R. Littler, 1985, Aldershot: Gower in association with the Open University, 161–71. See http://ieeecss.org/CSM/library/1981/sept/wo4-8.pdf, accessed December 16, 2014.

66. *VBL*, 2012, §44.

67. We are very grateful to Pierre Lecocq for the insights of this paragraph.

68. Charles S. Handy, *The Hungry Spirit: Beyond Capitalism; A Quest for Purpose in the Modern World* (New York: Broadway Books, 1999), 239.

69. Peter F. Drucker and James C. Collins, *The Five Most Important Questions You Will Ever Ask about Your Organization* (New York: Leader to Leader Institute, 2008), xix. The view ("that people are an organization's most valuable resource") is "central to Peter Drucker's philosophy," xix.

70. Patricia Werhane, Margaret Posig, Lisa Gundry, Laurel Ofstein, and Elizabeth Powell, *Women in Business: The Changing Face of Leadership* (Westport, CT: Praeger Publishers, 2007), 75.

71. Hittinger explains that "In papal teachings since Pius XI, subsidiarity is proposed as a principle of non-absorption, not a principle that necessarily requires devolution. As it is commonly understood, *devolution* is the opposite of subsidiarity. For devolution presupposes either: (a) an ontological deficiency, measured by a kind of cost-benefit analysis, or (b) that the central government rightly possesses a plenary power

that it has now decided to redistribute to other powers and authorities" ("Pluralism and Subsidiarity," 395).

72. Peter F. Drucker, *The Effective Executive: The Definitive Guide to Getting the Right Things Done* (New York: HarperCollins, 2006), 37–38.

73. Charles B. Handy, *The Age of Paradox* (Boston: Harvard Business School Press, 1994), 146.

74. For examples in health care, see Sr. Patricia Talone, "Principle of Subsidiarity: Challenges and Opportunities in Today's Health Care Environment," *Health Care Ethics USA* 16, no. 2 (Spring 2008), accessed December 16, 2014, http://www.chausa.org/docs/default-source /general-files/a557a5d13d7c42de96a80cbaa98278e31-pdf.pdf?sfvrsn=0. See also Bill Brinkman, "A Personal Reflection on our Future Leaders," *Health Progress* (July–August 2014), accessed December 16, 2014, http://www.chausa.org/publications/health-progress/article/july -august-2014/a-personal-reflection-on-our-future-leaders.

75. Mary Elsbernd, OSF, "Theoretical Foundations of Interactive Leadership in Catholic Social Teachings," accessed December 18, 2014, http:// www.stthomas.edu/media/catholicstudies/center/johnaryaninstitute /conferences/1997-antwerp/Elsbernd.pdf. Paper presented in 1997 at a University of St. Thomas Conference, accessed December 18, 2014, http://www.stthomas.edu/cathstudies/cst/research/conferences /antwerp/acceptedpapers/.

76. T. Dean Maines, "Self-Assessment and Improvement Process for Organizations," *The Palgrave Handbook of Spirituality and Business,* ed. Luk Borkaert and Laszlo Zsolnai (New York: Palgrave MacMillan, 2011), 359–68. See also, Goodpaster, Maines, and Weimerskirch, "A Baldrige Process for Ethics?" and Kenneth E. Goodpaster, T. Dean Maines, and Michelle Rovang, "Stakeholder Thinking: Beyond Paradox to Practicality," *The Journal of Corporate Citizenship* 7 (Autumn 2002): 93–111. Reprinted in *Unfolding Stakeholder Thinking* (Sheffield Greenleaf, 2002) by Jörg Andriof.

77. This line of question was given to us by Pierre Lecocq, CEO of Inergy Automotive in conversations.

78. Stephen R. Covey, "Three Roles of the Leader in the New Paradigm," *The Leader of the Future: New Visions, Strategies, and Practices for the Next Era*, ed. Frances Hesselbein, Marshall Goldsmith, and Richard Beckhard (San Francisco: Jossey–Bass, 1996), 149–59.

79. Handy, *The Age of Unreason*, 127.

80. See Robert G. Kennedy, *The Good That Business Does* (Grand Rapids, MI: Acton Institute, 2006), 68.

81. See Dorothy Day, *The Long Loneliness: The Autobiography of Dorothy Day* (New York: Harper, 1952), 171.

— NOTES —

— NOTES —